Shark Squadron Pilot

By

Bert Horden

Shark Squadron Pilot – Bert Horden

First publication in Great Britain

© Herbert A Horden 2002

First edition published in 2002 by:

Independent Books
3 Leaves Green Crescent
Keston
Bromley
BR2 6DN
United Kingdom

Tel: (UK) 01959 573360
Fax: (UK) 01959 541129

e-mail mail@independentbooks.co.uk

Edited by Richard Munro and Peter Osborne

Designed by Peter Osborne

Jacket illustrations by Jim Petrie

ISBN: 1 872836 45 3

Contents

FOR MY LOVELY FAMILY

DEDICATION

This book is dedicated to the pilots and
men of the Shark Squadron who gave
their lives so that we may enjoy freedom and, hopefully, long lasting peace

FOREWORD

The following true story was first written in 1973 from my diary, logbook and memory of the war years. It is surprising that as one gets older, longer term memories can remain quite clear even if yesterday's events are fuzzy. With this in mind I have only included events that are clear in my diary or logbook and of which I have a clear memory.

I carried out 130 'operations' or 'sorties' against the enemy. Some were full of action, many of which I have included. Others were routine and without incident (although we got shot at on most ops) and these I have omitted. These are just my experiences. The other pilots on 239 Wing had just as adventurous a time as I did.

It was fortunate for me to have been a 'fighter-bomber' pilot (fighter aircraft carrying bombs) on close army support as I believe it gave me a closer look at the 'sharp end' of the war than that experienced by many other RAF aircrew. I took a Kodak camera with me into the RAF, one that unfolded allowing bellows to be extended; the early photographs were taken with this. Later, as the text will explain, I acquired a Leica 35mm with which I took dozens of black and white photographs as colour film was not available to me at that time. I couldn't get the films developed and printed in Italy, so I brought them all home and had them done in England at great expense but well worth it. Some others shown here were taken by fellow pilot, 'Matt' Matthias, who kindly obtained copies for any of us who wanted them. Matt was killed in action with the Squadron in April 1945 in northern Italy.

With rockets in space and nuclear weapons abounding there will never be another war like WWII. Hopefully the horrors of nuclear wars will discourage any country from starting one in the future but there always seems to be some insane leader who wants to cause chaos.

BERT HORDEN - October 2002

CHAPTER ONE

FROM DAD'S ARMY TO ROYAL AIR FORCE

In 1938 it was a bit posh to have a radio as not many could afford one. 'Radio for the Million' was the name of a DIY radio kit and my brother John and I built it from a box of valves, resistors, other components and a metal chassis. We followed the instructions carefully and when we first switched it on it worked. Father was so amazed he immediately set about making a wooden box for it, with beading round the edges. It was on this family radio in Bromsgrove that we heard the declaration of war on 3 September 1939. It was also on this radio that I heard the first call for volunteers for the Local Defence Volunteers (LDV): "Report to your nearest police station". As this was only twenty yards around the corner, I was first there.

We stood on guard duty for hours at Jackson's Farm with pick-axe handles. The biggest excitement was killing a rat that ran back and forth across my toes. My first effort at a deflection shot! We played Halfpenny Nap and slept on the bare floorboards. Later we were issued with second-hand .300 rifles from America and actually fired them at the butts. First World War veteran snipers thought they would show us young ones the way to do it and were mortified to find that we were the better shots. At first I thought what a good shot I was but later I realised that these old boys' eyesight was not as good as it had been in 1916!

I worked in the Municipal Gas Department in Birmingham after cycling the nine miles to save the bus fare. With this bit of spare cash I would play hookey from Building-Drawing at night school and visit the local Music Hall to see the likes of Max Miller who seemed very naughty – especially to me as a son of the Manse. He would come onto stage with a big ham held out in his left hand. "This is Hitler's left leg." Off he'd go to return with the ham in his right hand. "This is Hitler's right leg." Off he would go to return with a rod and two potatoes hanging from it. There would be a long pause while the audience roared its head off, and then, with perfect timing, "No you're wrong, they're King Edwards". More roars of laughter.

The Battle of Britain raged and I decided I wanted to become a fighter pilot. Air raids over the city were frightening. I joined the office Air Raid Precautions (ARP) team and put out incendiary bombs on the roof by dropping my tin hat over them and then using a stirrup pump. One night a bomb dropped on the front of these Gas Offices, blowing stone columns across the road and killing six of our team. I had just popped down to the canteen for a mug of cocoa.

I cycled more because the buses to Bromsgrove were crowded with pushing and shoving women and children trying to escape the night raids.

Mac, a friend in the office, told me he had been accepted as a navigator in the Fleet Air Arm. He said that in the Navy he would be captain of the aircraft. He ran the complaints counter and telephone in the public area of the offices. When he left I got his job. He said, "Bert, there's only one instruction to give you and you'll cope all right. When a complainant rings," he explained, "just get the name and address. Trouble is they go on and on and on: 'the smell's awful, the cat's been sick, daren't light the fire' and so on. All you have to do," says Mac, "is butt in with 'Hello, hello, hello – oh dear, we've been cut off' and put the phone down". This has been a useful tip for me ever since.

There were lots of war jokes around the office, like the Japanese one-man suicide submarines which all had a notice over the little entrance hole, 'Mind Your Head'.

I studied aircraft recognition and learnt that RAF squadron leaders earned £2,000 per year. As I was earning about £175 this seemed a fortune.

At last I was accepted as potential aircrew for the RAF and went to be attested at Cardington in Bedfordshire. I really meant it when I swore allegiance to King George VI on a tattered copy of the Bible. After a week or so of anxious anticipation at home in February 1941, I was posted to

Babbacombe, Devon to start life in the RAF.

I met some young men on the train, all hoping to become Spitfire pilots, and with eager anticipation. I was posted here to be kitted out as an AC2 by the tailor. Surprisingly everything fitted reasonably well. The only problem was with the forage cap, known to the RAF by another name closely related to a certain intimate part of a lady's anatomy. Unfortunately my parting was on the wrong side. I had to go to the barber to get it changed. For years my hair stood up on end in protest, despite liberal helpings of Brylcreem.

The highlight of this week was being marched to a cinema in Babbacombe to have a motivating talk by Johnnie Johnson VC. We just couldn't wait to be heroes.

When Friday night came we were told to have the week-end off, back on Monday by 6 am. Loud cheers. However, a crafty sergeant explained to us that we must be on Church Parade on Sunday morning. Our names would be read out from a list and woe betide anyone missing. There was one possible way out of this, he went on; if we wanted our names deleted from the list he would need 2/6 d (12.5 pence) from each of us. The desire to show off my new uniform to family, friends and girl friends outweighed the desire to hold on to the half-crown, so slipped it into his palm, made sure he knew my name and set off for the station. This was quite frightening. After all I had sworn allegiance at Cardington and here I was after only a few days in the Service, going AWOL. Whatever would become of me? Would I be shot as a deserter? Felt better on the train heading north eastwards. Unfortunately, I had to change at Bristol Temple Meads for the Birmingham train. There was a long wait and, being among a swirling mass of Service people, I thought I would sit at a table in the buffet with some curly sandwiches and a cuppa. I only sat a minute when two burly RAF policemen sat at the very same table. I could almost hear the firing-squad taking aim. As soon as I could, without looking guilty, I took off rapidly to a distant part of the platform to await the train.

Everyone was duly impressed by the uniform, so it was almost worthwhile. After another nervous wait of a few days, my posting to No 8 ITW (Initial Training Wing) at Newquay, Cornwall, arrived and it was to last from March to May 1941. Here we began to learn the laws, rules and customs of the RAF. We were instructed in how to fill up the necessary forms showing next of kin and other information. If we got it wrong the NCO told us in no uncertain terms what he would stick in our ears and do for not listening. Again, as a son of the Manse, this all came as a bit of a shock.

We learnt how to strip a gas-operated machine gun, how to dig a deep-trench latrine, how to spit and polish our boots and how to march with or without gas masks. I enjoyed PT (Physical Training) on the beach and even swimming in the sea (yes, in March!). I had never been so fit before or since, despite learning to smoke and drink. Best of all, I guess, was learning the principles of flight.

We were billeted in hotel rooms in the Crescent right on the sea front. Iron bedsteads, mattress and rough blankets were all right as we slept like logs and got up at the crack of dawn.

Aircrew cadets at ITW Newquay March 1941. Left to right: Self, Grahme Rosser, Pat Halliday and John Myers

Initial Training Wing, Newquay 1941. Proud of our new flying kit.
Centre Pat Halliday, to his left John Myers and on his right self.

A coach took us to RAF St. Eval just along the coast, where we saw Spitfires, Hudsons and even a helicopter, all close to. We talked to the pilots who learnt where we were billeted and promised us a visit. As good as their word, three Spits flew right down on the sea straight towards our cliff-top billet, pulling up just in time over our roof with that wonderful roar of Merlin engines. No doubt the authorities took a dim view of this caper but we loved it. Later the Spits from St. Eval did a toilet roll raid over the town centre of Newquay. We thought it good fun but the Mayor was not amused.

Aircrew training took place in Canada, USA, Rhodesia, South Africa as well as in England, therefore there was much speculation as to where we would be sent.

Then came the posting to the transit camp at West Kirby in the Wirral and being kitted out with tropical gear – so "look out Africa, here we come". Enemy air raids over Liverpool prevented us exploring the night-life there and West Kirby had none, so we were impatient for our boat. We wanted desperately to be flying. Eventually it came and on 28th June we embarked on HMT Rangitata.

HMT Rangitata, July 1941. Our troopship from Scotland to Cape Town

CHAPTER TWO

HMT RANGITATA

As we sailed around Northern Ireland and into the Atlantic in His Majesty's Troopship no one was allowed on deck. We all slept below in hammocks or on the lower deck floors. It seemed as though I was the only one not seasick. The fetid smell of diesel oil, lack of light, cigarette smoke and crowded conditions made it the most uncomfortable week or so of my life. The dreadful conditions seemed to lower everyone's standard of honesty, as kit was stolen willy-nilly from one person to another. Rumours of troopship sinkings added dread to discomfort. As we passed by the Bay of Biscay weather conditions worsened and many were very ill. It nearly cured me of smoking but unfortunately not quite.

As we got further south towards north-west Africa things got better. We were allowed up on deck for short periods to lean over the rail and watch the flying fish, porpoises and, at night, the magnificent show of florescence in the wake of the ship. At night no smoking – no matches – no light of any sort. Soon sleeping on the deck was allowed, but only for the fortunate few who, like me, bagged a place and stuck to it day and night. We must have been only a hundred or two out of two thousand who fought for this breather on deck. The trouble was, one only had to go to the toilet (not a happy experience anyway) to find one's place taken by a usurper who would fight rather than give up his ill-gotten place.

It was in these circumstances that four of us cadets formed what was to be my first lasting friendships of the war. We four kept our side-by-side places on deck by defending them against any intruder while one of us was away. In this way we enjoyed some air, a sea view and relative comfort. Unfortunately the crew hosed the decks down every morning at first light. We had to gather up our blankets and try to stand out of the way. When they had gone we rushed back to retake our wet places and dry out our boots and socks.

We four were a mixed bunch, the leader being John Myers. He was streetwise and took me under his wing realising that I had had a relatively narrow upbringing. His father was a successful businessman in Leeds. His family lived at Headingly overlooking the cricket field and could see play from the bedroom windows. All very sophisticated.

Pat Halliday was the fighting Irishman. It was amazing how he could develop a simple discussion into an argument and then into fisticuffs. One day he picked a fight with one of the crew who hosed down Pat's bedding before he had time to lift it out of the way. This proved to be a mistake as the crew overpowered him and he ended up in irons. It took the remaining three of us two days to persuade the captain to release him.

'Doc' Stewart was the gentleman. I couldn't imagine him killing Huns, yet he was as keen as any of us to have a go. He was a medical student determined to become a qualified doctor as soon as the war was over. Graham Rosser was the Welshman, always singing his way through life and brightening us all up accordingly.

As we reached sunnier climes off the west coast of Africa, life became more pleasant and the fear of torpedoing lessened. We swapped paperbacks to read away the hours. My favourite was 'No Orchids for Miss Blandish' – a rather risqué novel of the time. The regular RAF NCOs (Non-commissioned officer) surfaced and started housey-housey games on deck. A lot of money changed hands and I learned the meaning of 'Doctors Delight', 'Two Fat Ladies', 'Clickety Click' and so on, mostly as a spectator. As we earned about 2/6 d (12.5 p) per day we didn't really have any spare money.

It was about this time that we learned that our sister ship had become detached from the convoy and had been sunk by a German U-Boat. Those not drowned had been picked up by other ships. There was a number of aircrew cadets like ourselves among them.

Our first port of call was Freetown, Sierra Leone. We were not allowed ashore but could barter for delicious fruits from the natives clamouring around the Rangitata in their canoe-like craft. They could also dive and catch sixpenny coins (2.5p) thrown into the water. Here we took on board a share of the RAF survivors of the sinking. They were badly shaken but full of fantastic stories of survival. Doc Stewart was in his element ministering to their minor injuries. Pat Halliday refrained from arguing with them. Graham kept singing 'A Nightingale Sang in Berkeley Square' and all was happiness.

The 'Crossing the Line' ceremony added to the fun. Most of us got lathered with sea-water soap and chucked into the tiny pool on top deck, as was the custom. We had picked up good food supplies at Freetown so we enjoyed a better standard of eating especially compared with the dreadful shortages back in England. Now we could look forward to some flying. Home, with its narrow way of life and food shortages seemed far away to me. Freedom!

The famous Table Mountain came into view with Devil's Peak at its side, so at last we knew our destination: Cape Town. We all wanted to go ashore. We had been about six weeks at sea. However the authorities thought otherwise. Now a queue started to the Officer in Charge to explain why each had a very special compassionate reason to go ashore: "My auntie Maude lives in Cape Town" and so on. Of our four, only Pat was allowed ashore. We never did find out what tall story he told but his Irish blarney saw him through and he had a good evening ashore. In the morning we all trooped off the ship and straight into waiting trains heading for Bulawayo, Rhodesia (now Zimbabwe).

The train was heaven compared to the boat. It took us two days and two nights. At every stop, and there were many, kind ladies served tea and cakes and coloured boys sold us exotic fruits for pennies. A shilling would buy a whole sack of oranges. We slept in bunk beds and walked along the corridor to the dining car for our meals, a shift at a time. All was excitement at getting nearer and nearer to actual flying.

Hillside Camp near Bulawayo consisted of rows of straw huts with wooden boards and palliasses to sleep on, about twenty to a hut. No doors, only doorways, but the climate was perfect. During the day we wore khaki shorts and shirts plus bush jackets in the evening. I can't remember wearing topees but we did have them.

Hillside Camp Bulawayo, Rhodesia, September 1941
Aircrew Cadet billets

The food was great with lots of exotic fruits such as guavas. The ladies in the canteen advised us to drink lime and lemonade rather than milk to avoid thickening the blood in the hot climate. We went into town to find wide roads and modern buildings. Cecil Rhodes had insisted on roads wide enough for a sixteen oxen wagon team to turn around. The coloured natives had to step off the pavement to let us whites pass. The black boys who cleaned our huts were afraid to fraternize. We couldn't see how it could last, but it did last for many years as you will know.

The white Rhodesians were friendly but kept us at arm's length. Apparently, early war RAF personnel had been overwhelmed with parties and general hospitality but had not behaved well – like seducing the daughters and peeing in the flower vases. This was not the sort of behaviour the locals expected from the RAF 'heroes' from the UK. It was not surprising then that we had a cool reception.

Hillside Camp, native workmen building new billets

Eighth Avenue, Bulawayo, showing Barclay's Bank, Supreme Court and Cecil Rhodes Monument

Daytime lectures concentrated on theory of flight and allied subjects so we paid close attention. The Flight Sergeant who introduced us to the training schedule fancied himself as a Professor Higgins and could place our accents with precision. He got us to stand up one by one and say a few sentences. From this he told us where we came from – almost to the street. He had got Pat Halliday weighed up: father from Dublin, mother from Limerick, grandmother from Scotland and so on. He was so very, very clever we began to wonder if he had been having a careful look at our record papers. We never really knew.

The white Rhodesians enjoyed a very high standard of living including a new car (mostly American) every year. They used to pay a second-hand car dealer to take away the old ones and he had a large store full of them. When the RAF turned up it was a heaven-sent opportunity to get rid of them at a good profit. John Myers could drive a car, of course. I'd never even sat in a driver's seat. He persuaded me to go halves on a Chevy with a 'dickey seat' at the back – all open top, of course. The total price paid was £10.

'Maisie' the Chevvy with author at the helm. She seated
four with two in the 'dickey seat' at the back

'Maisie' on the road to Matopos Hills, site of the grave of Cecil Rhodes

So that's how I came to own my first half motorcar which I couldn't drive. John was so busy with a variety of girl friends he had acquired in quick time, that he didn't have time to teach me to drive. "Tomorrow, Bert, tomorrow. I've got a date tonight." I got exasperated and demanded a share of the car on alternate evenings. On my evenings I climbed in and pressed various pedals to see what happened until I got the hang of it. There was very little traffic and only blacks needed provisional or full licences. It must have been quite a sight – a Chevy with hiccups jerking along with a young airman struggling with the steering wheel. I could get along provided I concentrated fixedly on what to do next, so thought I would take a girl out for a ride. John had a spare one, so it was arranged. It was not a very successful evening. She complained bitterly that I was more interested in making the car do what I wanted than her! I never did have a driving lesson. We decided to call the car 'Maisie'. I suspect it was in memory of one of John's more successful forays into the local civilian social life.

CHAPTER THREE

THE SCREAM OF DEATH
AND THE GOLD MINE

All four of us were posted to 27 EFTS (Elementary Flying Training School), Induna, near Bulawayo, to start our flying careers. The excitement was intense. At last we were to fly. We were all very excited and with a dread of not succeeding. A sad incident marred our first day at this school. To get as near as possible to the aeroplanes we crowded onto the fringe of the flying field to watch pupils of the previous course do their 'circuits and bumps'. We could see the accident about to happen – a pupil landed but for some reason did not taxi away. We could see another solo pupil about to land on top of him. Our shouts were to no avail, of course. The petrol tank of a Tiger Moth is in the top wing and it was ruptured by the one smashing down on top of it – bursting into flames and trapping the first pupil in his cockpit. The pilot of the second Tiger climbed out but there was no way he could penetrate the flames to release his colleague whose screams could be heard by all of us as he died. When we eventually got near we were all crying. We got the shock out of our systems by talking about it for hours in the mess.

The next day was my first ever flight in an aeroplane – a Tiger Moth biplane. The instructor was gentle and helpful; a wonderful experience to remember always. The second day the instructor did a loop and dust and dirt from the cockpit floor got in my eyes. I was told not to grumble but clean it out before the next trip, an unpleasant task standing on one's head in the cockpit with damp cloths. So we began to learn to fly.

Weather conditions were perfect but for one quirk – once or twice the wind became so strong that by throttling back a little the Tiger would gain no headway and even 'go backwards'. It was possible, but not popular with instructors, to take off, throttle back at 100 ft (30 m) and sink gently down to the ground again. I learned some of the tricks of airmanship such as being at all times prepared for a forced landing into the wind by watching its direction on long grasses or cows facing into it.

Failure at this time would be worse than death to any of us. This dreaded end came to friend Graham Rosser – he was airsick. The moment the wheels left the ground he was ill. His instructor gave him every chance but to no avail, so he could never become aircrew at all and we had to say goodbye. Result – the rest of us tried even more desperately to succeed. I had a serious problem myself – trying to land 30ft under ground or 30ft above ground. I was the despair of my instructor who transferred me to 'X' Flight which was for pupils with some potential but with a major problem.

I couldn't sleep for tossing and turning in fear of failure. Now I owe a huge debt to Flying Officer Cousins, my new instructor. He knew just what to do. He taxied to the far edge of the field and got out leaving his parachute. I didn't know what was coming. He leaned into the cockpit. "Horden, you will something well sit there till you get it into your something, something thick skull that the aircraft lands in the exact position you are in now. Look at the horizon and the attitude of the aircraft to it and something well sit there till I come back." With that, he walked back to the flight hut leaving me sitting in the hot sun for what seemed like an hour. I must have got it through my something thick skull because when he eventually got back and gave me a last chance to try a landing – thank God I could do it. I made a spot-on landing and, after a few more, he let me go solo.

We studied hard whenever we were not flying; no parties, no visits out, just aeroplanes, aeroplanes and more aeroplanes. Altogether I did seventy-three hours flying Tiger Moths, thirty of them solo. I didn't like night flying much – I always felt disorientated by about 3 am. I never did get used to it. Night navigation was not the best skill of one of our colleagues. He was supposed to be up solo for an hour. After three hours, and he didn't turn up, we knew he must have had a problem. He was found the next day in a two-foot deep hole without his parachute which was half a mile away. It was presumed he had run out of fuel, baled out, and turned the knob on his harness and given it a bang (as we did to get out of the harness after every trip, of course) instead of releasing the 'chute by pulling the D ring.

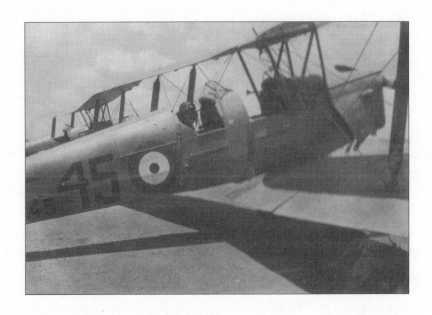

DeHavilland Tiger Moth, Induna Elementary
Flying Training School, Rhodesia

Solo flying was wonderful. The only clouds about were the occasional fluffy cumulous and they were a delight for flying above, around and among. I felt close to God. What bliss! It was summed up perfectly by a poem written by Cadet (later Air Vice-Marshal) Brian Young:

How can they know the joy to be alive
Who have not flown?
To loop and spin, and roll and climb and dive
The very sky one's own.
The surge of power as engines race,
The sting of speed,
The rude wind – buffet on one's face,
To live indeed!

I loved it so much that I made up for the early problem and was given an 'above average' assessment of ability as a pilot. However, the entry in my log book also asks "Has he shown aptitude as a pilot navigator?" Answer: "No"! This was very shrewd, as it was to show up later when leading a fighter squadron. My men grumbled that I had not taken the quickest route back to base. I tried not to let on but the truth was I was nearly lost and only a lucky landmark showing up got me and the squadron back at all!

We did get the occasional trip out in Maisie the Chevy. Having taught myself to drive I was eager to show off to the others, so I set off as driver to take four of us to the Matopas Hills and Rhodes' grave for a Sunday afternoon out along the two narrow strips of tarmac that served as a road (see page 21). We hadn't gone very far when there was a smell of burning. They shouted at me to stop. Then flames leapt up from the front floorboards. I'd left the parking brake on and the whole thing was red hot! We were out in the bundu (bush) – no water for miles, not even a flask of tea. There was only one way to put out the fire and save Maisie! We reckoned the cloud of steam lingered for hours!

I was at No 22 SFTS Thornhill, Gwelo, Rhodesia from January to April 1942.

Here we were given the rank of Acting Sergeant Unpaid living in the Sergeants' Mess. Anyway, it was promotion and, like one AC2 said to the other AC2, "Only 13 promotions and we shall be Air Marshals".

Now we were to fly 2-seater low-wing monoplanes called Harvards. Powerful stuff compared with Tigers. These aeroplanes' propellers made a lovely cracking sound when passing at right angles to one's ears. Only six hours flying to solo. I was getting near to a real fighter aircraft now. There were no accidents to mar this course and the weather was still perfect.

North American Harvard air-to-air. Formation flying, Senior Flying Training School, Thornhill, Gwello, Rhodesia

I was chosen as pupil/second pilot to go with the Flight Commander to see his girlfriend in Bulawayo, landing at Induna, which gave me a chance to chat up my old instructors and say a thank you. I flew the Harvard both ways and made good landings which is perhaps why I got another 'above average' at the half way stage through the course. This was vitally important because getting one's Wings was dependent on it. The snag was our whole course got such terrible results in the meteorology exam that they failed us en masse and kept us in for hours and hours on a cram course for us to try again. We tried a system of cribs to make sure we passed but got found out. Eventually most of us passed the re-set exam and, a great day, I was presented with the coveted Wings, officially known as 'The Flying Badge'. It went over the left top pocket and couldn't be taken away unless the owner went LMF (Lack of Moral Fibre). Also, I was commissioned and had to buy a new uniform, but the Wings meant the most.

To make sure we didn't think we knew it all, we had another seventy hours flying to complete the course. Now learning combat techniques including formation flying, air to ground firing, low flying, high dive-bombing (smoke bombs), floodlight landings, photography, low level formation bombing, fighter-bomber tactics as well as a lot of instrument flying. Air-to-ground firing was into floating targets on a lake, called 'splash targets' because we could see where the bullets were going and hopefully improve aim. The lake was infested with crocodiles and when instructors were not around the crocs got more attention than the target!

My last solo trip at this school was formation flying. I was determined to get a close up photograph of a flying Harvard, so secreted my camera in the cockpit. I thought it very daring to get wing tip inside wing tip and hold the joystick between my knees while taking a snapshot. After all that the print came out looking not so close and nearly off the picture at the bottom left.

Towards the end of this course the CO chose me to fly him to Belvedere (N'Saka) in Northern Rhodesia (now Zambia) on a diplomatic mission to the politicians of that country. I put on my best bush jacket and shorts, all spruced up and off we went with me in the back cockpit. I had to hang around at Belvedere for about four hours before his lordship was ready to return to base looking slightly flushed from a good lunch. All went well until I came to retract the wheels on take off. Suddenly the flaps came down and I had a job to keep the Harvard climbing. Got a rocket from his lordship on the intercom: "What the hell —" etc, etc. I didn't realize till I had time to think about it that my sleeve (I had never flown in a jacket before) had caught on the flap lever. Too late – his lordship was not interested in excuses. I reckon that's why he gave me only an 'average' assessment on completion of the course.

Social life at SFTS improved especially after the 'Wings' ceremony, mostly because I got invited into the civilian society. It happened like this: I was leaving camp on foot one evening and had signed out at the Guard Room. I had only gone a few yards when a man about my age caught up with me and said he had signed out under my name which was the same as his. As Horden is an uncommon name we chatted, became friends and eventually discovered that we were related. Cecil Horden was in the Rhodesian Army Medical Corps and with his brother, a cripple from an accident, ran a small two-stamp gold mine. He took me to see the mine which started above ground but sloped underground where there were caverns of various sizes and a couple of Matabeles (local tribesmen) digging out rich gold-veined quartz. He gave me a lump to keep. As we got deeper into the mine with his torch leading the way, he suddenly lighted on a snake curled up on a ledge. Without warning he drew a pistol and fired several shots at it. He killed the snake. That was all right but the bullets ricocheting around the cavern seemed to me more dangerous than the snake – I suppose he knew best. While I was there, they had struck it rich – took a lot of money from the assay office – and set about spending it in great style. They each bought a huge new Cadillac. When I was not flying, I was included in the parties and a great time was had by all. Before I left they had run out of money, the mine had filled up with water and they were trying to borrow pumps from friends to dry it out and hopefully start again. Cecil took me to see his father in Salisbury who had a family tree from Somerset House. There we discovered that we were relatives, both being connected to a Bishop Horden of Exeter. At the top of this family tree was an illegitimate son of Robert Bruce. I have a feeling half the UK population is descended from this active gentleman.

Cecil Horden's two-stamp gold mine near Salisbury Rhodesia 1942

I had my 21st birthday about this time – more parties. I also learnt to enjoy eating fried locusts. You have to pull their legs and wings off first. I went to Victoria Falls for the day out. There was not a lot of water at that time of year but I was duly impressed by the majesty of it all.

At the end of the course there was exciting news. We were all to be posted back to Blighty. I was just about to pack my kit when I fell ill and had to go to the sick-bay with malaria. Most of my course came to say goodbye. They were as pleased as punch to be going home. I felt sicker still. As it happened Cecil Horden was the orderly on duty and he soon got me fit again, only to be told I had to go to the Middle East via a train to Durban to await a boat. I was upset at the time but now have no regrets. After all, I am alive. I never met any of them again but I did hear that John Myers was killed over Germany flying a bomber. I sold Maisie for a fiver and boarded the train.

_____

CHAPTER FOUR

SOUTH AFRICA TO EGYPT

I arrived at the Clairwood transit camp, Durban, without knowing anyone. There were Army and Navy as well as Air Force officers, all awaiting a boat to the Middle or Far East. I met a subaltern who had been at Kingswood School, Bath, with me. His name was Close and we had both voted Communist in the school mock elections just to be awkward, so we were both rebellious blokes. He wasn't happy with the army or the idea of fighting the Japs. I had a few drinks with him. The local brandy was 4d (less than 2 pence) per generous tot and we ate little bananas at 2d per bunch, known as 'Lady's Fingers'. He said he had local contacts so off he went into the town. Later I thought I had better see what Durban was like, walking up and down the promenade for some time, then recced the town centre. At about dusk I found the Starlight Club, which seemed to be the drinking centre for service people of all sorts and ranks. Drinks were nearly as cheap as in the Camp so I settled down at a table on my own.

The novelty of this club was that the domed roof opened like an observatory to reveal a starlit sky. If it clouded over, the roof was closed over to show imitation stars anyway, so it was always starlit. I was getting a bit bored when I saw subaltern Close sitting not far away with two girls! He caught my eye and beckoned me over to join them. Here was natural congenial company and we enjoyed exchanging experiences and our different ways of life. The girls knew all the troopship movements which were supposed to be highly secret. They told Close that his boat for the Far East was the day after next and that my boat wouldn't be for a couple of weeks. Both forecasts proved to be very accurate.

That evening I was invited by one of the girls back home for some supper in a luxurious penthouse. Her mother and father were totally pro-British (not all South Africans were – more later) and offered wonderful hospitality. I was to regard their home as my own. Her father owned a garage/service station in Queen Street and told me to call in the morning to be fixed up with a car and petrol. His daughter was in a social circle of young people and she would introduce me around. What luck!

The next morning I left camp right after roll-call for the garage where the father lent me an Oldsmobile saloon and told the 'boy' on the pumps to fill it up as often as I wanted and put it on his personal account. Unfortunately, I had to sleep at Clairwood and report for roll-call each morning as we may have had to embark any day. With the car this was easy but I had to be careful about giving lifts. There had been some beat-ups of Brits by local Dutch political party members calling themselves *Ossewa Brandwarg*. They wore beards and their chief aim was to get the British out of the Union of South Africa as soon as possible. They got decoys without beards to stop a car, open a door and beat up the occupants.

I took a carload of South Africans to Brighton Beach just down the coast for a party. Next morning I was told to stay in camp indefinitely. It looked like a couple of great weeks in Durban were at an end, so I told the garage to come and take the car back. I was told the boat would be ready the next day and, sure enough, I embarked on HMT Nieu Amsterdam. The Lady in White singing 'Land of Hope and Glory' was on the quayside to see us off which she did for every troopship. On this trip I had an officer's cabin and bathroom. It was very pleasant all the way up the Gulf of Suez to Port Taufiq to a world of Arabs, bustling, shouting, begging, smelling, bargaining, selling everything from a comb to a little sister. Great nets full of kit bags and other luggage were hoisted from the hold on to lighters. I saw one whole net-full fall into the sea, wondering if mine was among it. Arabs said *"marleesh"* - difficult to translate but it summed up the general attitude - "Never mind – who cares anyway."

We were getting near to some action now. The Hun was advancing on Egypt from the Western Desert. I stayed at another transit camp, this time at Kasfereet, Egypt. Life in any of the services is nearly all waiting. This was when I really began to feel like an officer. I had to take parades of airmen fresh off troopships. Come to think of it, fresh was not the word. With the help of the MO, I had to get the clean ones to scrub the dirty ones under a tap. They had to be drilled, inspected and generally kept in order. Here was the first time I was 'Orderly Officer'. I went to the Airmen's Mess with my Sergeant who shouted "Orderly Officer! Any complaints?" One airman came back crisply "No complaints about this swill at all, sir". I thought it best to ignore this but thereafter never did like this recurring job. The MO issued large numbers of FFI kits (Free From Infection kits - for the prevention of venerial disease). I went into Cairo for the first time and sat in a restaurant having afternoon tea. On ordering a second cup, the waiter threw the dregs of the first straight under the table. When I exclaimed he just said *"marleesh"* - that word again.

A number of American aircrew arrived so I had some amusing company. Very soon I found myself talking with an American accent. I went together with these friends into Cairo along a dusty road for thirty miles. Over to the right, way out in the desert, was a pink castle like something out of Walt Disney shimmering in the hot sunshine. The story went that it contained a beautiful virgin princess guarded by fifty eunuchs. I spent the rest of the journey planning her downfall. I did the usual Sphinx, pyramids and riding on a flea-ridden camel. Beggars and shoeshine boys were a nuisance. If we didn't stop for a shine they would flick polish as you walked by in the hope that you would stop after all. This was especially nasty when wearing suede desert shoes, known as 'Brothel Creepers', and they splashed black polish. Thus animosity grew between service men and the street Arabs.

It was time to move on. I got posted to Heliopolis Airport – a brick built permanent RAF station – as Aerodrome Control Officer, there to await posting to OTU (Operational Training Unit). The reason for delay was that the Fighter OTU was being rapidly moved south to the Sudan, out of the way of the advancing Hun. There were three of us aerodrome control officers to run the watchtower. We worked two days on and one day off. There was not much activity at night so one stayed awake while the other slept. It was the central operational station for the Middle East and a hive of activity. Aircraft of all sorts were coming and going to keep us busy and interested. Churchill himself arrived in his Liberator which had been a present from Roosevelt. Many VIPs milled around. COs of desert squadrons used to nip in, in all types of aircraft, for meetings or a little nibble at the flesh-pots of Cairo.

The Germans came at night and dropped a few bombs but mainly when the sirens went it was a false alarm. One night some Junkers Ju 88s came and we covered our ears expecting the crump of bombs but there was just a whooshing noise. They had covered the airport with spikes. These always landed with one vicious spike sticking up with the idea of putting the airport out of action. We alerted the station CO who ordered every man on the station to find a box, bucket or other receptacle. At first light we organised two hundred men of all ranks to line up along one side to step forward carefully picking up every spike. The airport was only out of use for a few hours, by lunchtime we were operating normally again.

For night landings the airport used gooseneck flares lit with a box of matches. When the air-raid warning went one of us had to go out in our little Ford pick-up truck and bring them all in. Not very comfortable in the middle of an air-raid.

There was a flight of two high-altitude Spitfires operating a few yards from our watchtower. Their job was to intercept and shoot down the inevitable daytime *shufti*-kite (*shufti*-arabic for a look-see) that came with cameras at about 30,000 ft (9144 m) to see what was going on in and around Cairo. Weeks went by without success until one day, showing great physical fortitude, for it was cold and dangerous up there even without a German shooting, one Spit, wallowing in the rarefied atmosphere, gradually caught up with the German and shot him down. Great celebrations!

On my day off I cadged lifts in all sorts of aircraft just for the fun of it. A Blenheim bomber pilot said I could have a trip if I would lie down out of the way in the bomb aimer's position. As he took off I could see buildings coming up fast and, to put it mildly, I felt rather nervous. He just pulled over the top by inches bringing a great sigh of relief from me.

There was a little captured civilian German low-wing monoplane Messerschmitt, Me 108 called a *Taifun* (Typhoon). It was just like a car inside with a bench seat in the front and was great fun to fly although mostly as passenger. There were some ancient RAF aircraft still flying. The Middle East was the last place to receive new types. I even had a trip to Beirut in a Vickers Virginia. Several old high-wing monoplane bombers called Bombays were other aircraft still flying, usually as ambulances.

Messerschmitt Me 108 Taifun. A very advanced touring aircraft, years ahead of its time. Very similar to many modern types like the Robin HR100, Socata TB9 or Piper Arrow

Another interesting activity here was the import of Hurricanes, Spitfires and Kittyhawks. These came by boat to Takaradi on the west coast of Africa where they were assembled and then flown in formation, led by a Blenheim, over the jungle and other hazards, to Heliopolis where they were prepared for action in the Western Desert. The delivery pilots would then pile into the Blenheim to be flown back for another delivery.

The United States Army Air Force (USAAF) were beginning to arrive in Egypt as reinforcements. They seemed to be rolling in money and of course prices of nearly everything took off in consequence, so it didn't take long for the delivery pilots to realise that the price of gold, snake skins, watches and other goodies was five times higher in Cairo than in Takaradi. Hence there started a profitable smuggling route. At that time there were no Customs and Excise people at either end of it. One Polish pilot became a friend. He had started with only five pounds and bought a couple of watches, arranged with a Cairo market 'business man' to take all he brought at exactly twice what he had paid for it in Takaradi. Before I left Helio he was over £2,000 per trip carrying goodies in kit bags stuffed in the wing ammo boxes of Spits and even beside him in the cockpit.

I used to give him lifts to the gates of Helio airport in our pick-up truck, where he would off-load into a taxi and head off into Cairo. I did this small service for all the delivery pilots, however my Polish friend insisted on treating me to the night-life of Cairo when I was not on duty – and who was I to be churlish? One night an attempt to bludgeon us to the ground and take our all was made by some Arabs – what is today called a mugging. We had just alighted from a taxi, the driver of which quickly drove off when he saw what was afoot . My Polish friend was having none of it; leaping into action like John Wayne himself with a quick left hook to one and a right swing to another. This group of Arabs then realised that they had taken on more than they expected and scarpered. He told me later that he had learned to look after himself on the back streets of Warsaw.

After leaving Helio, I was not surprised to hear that a stop had been put to this exciting trade. A Spitfire had forced landed in a clearing in the jungle. A search party led by a very proper Squadron Leader had found the Spitfire and on taking it apart for recovery and transport through the trees, a great deal of gold was discovered in the wings. From then on Customs officials were employed at Helio.

A great centre of social activity for officers of all the services was, of course, Shepheards Hotel in Cairo. They enjoyed a good time there when on leave from the rigours of the desert campaign. I tried it myself on a couple of occasions but never stayed the night. One time stuffy senior army officers were horrified to see an RAF officer completely naked chasing a young female around the corridors – not the sort of conduct becoming one of His Majesty's officers, they said. The matter was referred to higher authority and a court martial ensued. However the RAF officer was found not guilty when he quoted King's Regulations, para 152, sub-section 2a, which clearly states that an officer should be dressed suitably for the sport in which he is engaged. Anyway, I'm sorry to say it wasn't me.

Another social centre, this time for all ranks and the local ladies, was Groppys the restaurant in central Cairo. Their tea and cakes were renowned throughout the Middle East. "See you in Groppys," became the cry. On days off, when I couldn't get any trips in aeroplanes, I would nip out to the Heliopolis Sporting Club only a few yards from the airport. All British officers were allowed membership. It was a social centre for local business people in their turbans, with a bar and superb swimming pool. I enjoyed it so much but had a guilty feeling that I should really be in the Western Desert doing my bit. However that was soon to come.

My fellow aerodrome control officers were pilots awaiting OTU like myself and we put a lot of pressure on the Group Captain CO of Helio to get us posted. Rommel had arrived within striking distance of Cairo, although his lines of supply were greatly extended. We began to hear of Field Marshal Montgomery and how he was planning to reverse the situation. Everyone seemed to gain heart from 'Monty' so we were not surprised when the Battle of Alamein commenced not many miles away in the desert. The old Bombays were fitted out as ambulances and it was our job to see them safely in and out of Helio to and from the front, carrying the many casualties. We arranged for motor ambulances to meet them at Helio and transport them to various hospitals in Heliopolis and Cairo – quite an organisation. At least we were doing something useful for the war effort while awaiting OTU.

Bombay bombers used as ambulances, Heliopolis Airport, Cairo, 1942

The Station Commander was Group Captain Horsley. It was he who could release us for posting to OTU when he was prepared to agree that we were not irreplaceable. He was adamant that all service men not on duty when the air-raid sirens were heard should go immediately to the shelters. That was all right but most alarms were false. The Hun bombers could be approaching but then veered off to a target elsewhere.

Now the officers' mess was very congenial and dinner in the evening was definitely to be looked forward to. First into the dining room got the best service. This evening then, just after dark, the sirens sounded and most people went down to the shelters. However, I was hungry and I felt sure it would be the usual false alarm, so I sat on the mess front doorsteps awaiting the all clear. It was dusk, all was quiet with no one around. I sat patiently. Then the phone in the mess hall rang. I was not supposed to be there so I thought it better not to answer. But it kept on ringing and ringing. I began to wonder if there was some emergency, so eventually I decided to answer it. A most kindly voice asked if that was the officers' mess. "Yes," says I. "And who is that?" asked the genial voice. "Flying Officer Horden," says I. The voice changed both in tone and volume, "Well what the hell are you doing there, Horden, when you should be in a shelter?! This is Group Captain Horsley and you will report to my office at 9 am tomorrow". We all make mistakes, especially when young.

I duly reported at 9am. My punishment was to spend my days off conducting a Court of Inquiry into the 'Case of the Drunken Doctors'. Worse still, my two colleagues got a posting back to 'Blighty' for OTU. These three MOs had really got plastered in Heliopolis town that evening and when they arrived back at the guardroom had become abusive, started peeing up against the guardroom door and generally became unpopular, especially as the guards had spent a lot of time polishing that particular door and keeping the place clean and tidy. They were not amused and it all ended up in fisticuffs and the docs locked up for the night.

The C of I meant me taking down reams and reams of evidence from everyone concerned, ready for the CO to decide if there should be a Court Martial. The raucous descriptions and revolting details that I had to write down were a real laugh, but I would rather have been at Operational Training Unit! "All right, Horden," says the CO. "You have done your penance – now you can go to OTU – but it will be in the Sudan."

CHAPTER FIVE

HURRICANES AND THE DINING-IN NIGHT

The journey from Cairo to the Sudan was pleasant and interesting. First by train then by paddle boat up the Nile. This was luxurious and interesting. It was a comfortable and leisurely journey with good service and good food, all in pleasant weather. I viewed Cleopatra's Palace half under water and other sights.

Cleopatra's Palace mostly under water. River Nile 1942

*Cruising up the Nile, November 1942. Paddle steamer
with freight barge towed alongside*

Wadi Halfa Station, Sudan Railways, November 1942

The only thing was that the war seemed a long way away as we journeyed south. Then there was a train journey through the Nubian Desert and the climate was getting warmer. A welcome overnight stop at Atbara gave us the opportunity for a refreshing swim in the Sporting Club pool – then back on the train to Sinkat in the Anglo–Egyptian Sudan, as it was then called. The final leg in a 3-ton truck to the RAF camp and airfield called Carthago made us realise how far we were from civilisation – not a town or even a village for many miles. The only people to be seen outside camp were the local Fuzzy-Wuzzys (Sudanese tribesmen with short 'fuzzy' hair) on camels.

Operational Training Unit, Carthago, Sudan - the officers' quarters

So now we could concentrate on flying again. It was called a "Fighter Course". There were two flights; one on Tomahawks (P-40s) with the aim of going onto Kittyhawks (also P-40s) in the desert war, the other on Hurricanes with a view to flying Spitfires in action. I was put on Hurricanes, much to my delight. First, however, I had to do a refresher course on Harvard trainers again. I suppose this was only reasonable after nearly five months with no official flying. Even the Harvard flying was exciting, learning fighter tactics such as formation flying, camera deflection shots in dog-fights, low flying, dive-bombing and so on.

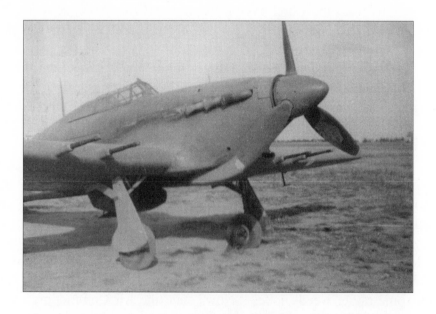

Hawker Hurricane at Carthago OTU. Ex-operational
aircraft used for training

On Christmas Eve 1942 I was ready for a first trip in a Hurricane. Of course there was only one seat, so I had to study the controls sitting in the cockpit on the ground with the 'Pilot's Notes'. No instructor would go with me this time – just me. The take-off was all right. I flew around for nearly an hour. Oh, joy – the most exhilarating flight of all. The Hurricane, although outshone in the public eye by the Spitfire, had actually shot down more 'Jerries' in the Battle of Britain and was a fine fighting aircraft. I got the feel of it quickly and enjoyed this first trip enormously. I had a bit of a problem coming in to land. I couldn't work out the little lights on the undercarriage controls and had to call up control on the radio and get instructions from the Chief Flying Instructor (CFI). Now all was OK. I came in to land cautiously, no doubt with the CFI and the instructor on the ground watching carefully. After a bit of a kangaroo landing, I was safe and sound on the ground. I taxied in expecting a rollicking from the CFI but he was understanding and said that calling for help had been the right thing to do. It was a wonderful feeling to have completed a first flight in a single-seat fighter. I had another hour's flight in the same 'Hurry' Mk I that day, feeling great. Then came two days off for Christmas.

As tradition demands, we officers served the airmen with their Christmas lunch followed, in the evening, by the Officers Dining-In Night. Come to think of it there was nowhere else to dine anyway. The Camp Commandant, an Air Commodore, sat at the head of the table with us junior officers at the bottom end. When the port had been passed around to the left and everyone was replete, the Air Commodore said he would like to hear a good story from anyone present. Some senior officers obliged with some rather weedy jokes. "Now," said the Air Commodore, "what about you at the other end of the table. Any stories?"

A Flight Lieutenant said he could contribute, so off he went. His story was that he had been stationed on a Spitfire flight in a jungle clearing in Burma. They were always on readiness. Often the klaxon would go; the pilots would snatch up their parachutes and scramble to the Spits ready to take off. Then it would be found to be a false alarm and they didn't have to take off. This happened many times and things got a little lax.

The Flight Lieutenant said between times he explored the jungle around the clearing and one day came across a baboon that seemed quite tame. After some time the baboon became friends with the pilots and started to copy their routine, such as putting on a parachute and running out to and climbing into a Spit. This was all right while they were all false alarms but one day the klaxon went; the pilots and the baboon ran out and climbed into the Spits. This time however it was the real thing and they all had to take off.

The officer telling the story then shut up and there were a few minutes silence. "Yes," asked the Air Commodore, "but what happened?" "Oh," said the Flight Lieutenant, "they got involved in a terrific dog-fight with some Jap Zeros". There were a few more moments of silence. "Yes," asked the Air Commodore, slightly exasperated, "but what happened to the baboon?" "Oh," said the Flight Lieutenant, "he survived all right and is now an Air Marshal!" Personally I think he would have liked to say the baboon was promoted to Air Commodore but didn't have the guts! Anyway, he got much laughter. I never saw the him again though.

Then I was back to flying Hurricanes. My next flight was up to 18,000 ft (5486 m) to become adept at using the oxygen bottles. The poor old 'Hurry' floundered from about 15,000 ft (4572 m) and it was extremely difficult to get to the full height.

Other flights included D/F homings, air to ground firing, formation flying, cine-gun attacks to be evaluated after the flight and so on. I enjoyed best the 'shadow firing'. Myself and another 'Hurry' flew out into the desert. One flew straight and level with its shadow scurrying over the sand. The other 'Hurry' fired deflection shots at the shadow and, of course, could see how good his aim was by the spurt of sand kicked up by the bullets. The first 'Hurry' had to be careful not to let his shadow cross over any camel-trains or other live obstacles.

One local camel owner came into camp complaining that his camel had been shot by one of our aircraft. The CO must have been very sympathetic to this Fuzzy-Wuzzy, giving him five pounds compensation – a fortune to the Fuzzy-Wuzzy. The trouble was, over the next week or two, a great queue of local camel owners formed outside the CO's office, all demanding five pounds for shot camels!

So sometimes we flew as far as the Red Sea near Port Sudan and the deserted city of Suakin and carried out our 'shadow-firing' over the water. The splashes from the bullets were just as effective. We were careful not to let the shadow fall over the local dhows but learnt to torment the poor sailors in another, less dangerous, way. By flying over a dhow at mast level and pulling up smartly at just the right moment, the slipstream got in its sails and rocked the boat alarmingly.. We weren't really wicked, just high spirited.

Two accidents marred this course slightly. Those Tomahawks had to be very careful to do front-wheel landings because when the tail-wheel touched the ground there was a nasty tendency for the aircraft to ground-loop, breaking the undercarriage. Unfortunately, one pilot failed to prevent this happening and his undercarriage gave way in the middle of the landing ground and he had to climb out and find his way back to the Flight hut on foot. A crane was in the middle of the landing ground trying to remove the broken aircraft when another Tomahawk pupil tried to take off. The high nose position on taxying and take-off, until the tail lifted, prevented the pilot seeing the crane before it was too late. He hit the crane and both aircraft burst into a ball of flame, incinerating the pilot.

Another Tomahawk plunged into the desert from a great height for some unknown reason. I was put in charge of the recovery party. We trundled over the desert in a 3-ton truck with an empty coffin bouncing about in the back. There was not much body to recover. I felt rather sick. We had to put stones in the coffin to make the weight seem right. We trundled back with these stones rattling about, for a funeral the next day.

Apart from this, I enjoyed my OTU on 'Hurrys' immensely and felt ready for an active squadron. I felt very confident, so was a little disappointed at the 'average' assessment entered in my logbook at the end of the course. I had flown 27.50 hours on Mark I Hurricanes and 2.10 hours on Mark IIs.

At this airfield there was just one Spitfire and I persuaded a Flying Officer instructor to let me fly it. I was only allowed a few minutes he said. I enjoyed about 20 minutes flying. The Spit was livelier and lighter to fly than the Hurricane and was not difficult as the controls and instruments were very similar. When I got down the instructor said he was afraid the CFI would be furious at him for letting me have a go and told me not to put it in my log book as the CFI would see it when he came to sign the book before I left. I would have liked more time to get acquainted with the Spit but it was not to be.

So it was I went back the same way to Cairo and the transit camp at Almaza. Surely, if there was any justice, I must be getting near to some real action this time?

———————————————

CHAPTER SIX

THE DESERT

LAST TRAINING BEFORE SQUADRON LIFE

Almaza was a dusty tented transit camp and landing ground not far from Cairo. When sandstorms blew up it was difficult to see the next tent. I reported in and was allocated a tent for two all to myself. Whenever possible I cleared off back to the Helio Sporting Club. Occasionally stopping part way at a coffee house where twice I sat a few tables away from the fat King Farouk and his retinue. I learnt to sing the bawdy song about him starting: "King Farouk, King Farouk, hang his bollocks on a hoook". I have forgotten the rest – probably just as well.

On the first night, back from an evening at Helio well lubricated, I found a body asleep on a camp bed in my tent. I kicked him awake. "What the hell —!" I discovered he was Johnnie Burcham also en route to a fighter squadron in the desert. Next day I introduced him to the joys of the Helio Sporting Club. I have kept in close touch with him for over fifty years now.

After a few days of this high life, there came through a posting to a Kittyhawk Wing for Johnnie and me. When the posting officer realised I had been on Hurricanes at OTU he sent me on a week's conversion course to an airfield near the [Suez] Canal called El Ballah. There I spent a week learning, again, to do front wheel landings on Harvards. Then, after studying the Pilot's Notes, I had my first flight in a Kittyhawk, another single-seat fighter. It is always exciting, a first trip in a different aircraft. I found it heavier to fly than a Hurricane and learnt that it was now used, in the desert, as a 'fighter–bomber', i.e. for dive bombing and strafing rather than just as a fighter, being no match for the German Me 109s or later the Fw 190s. It was an all-metal, sturdy, American-built aircraft that could take quite a beating – as I was to find out. Then I went back to Almaza for a few days before being sent into the desert.

Wellington bomber 'beating up' Almaza transit camp near Cairo

I went out to a birthday party with a crowd of young servicemen and some locals, followed by a trip to the cinema. A young lady invited Johnnie and me to dinner with her mother and father living in a top-storey flat in Helio. Father was a regular RAF Squadron Leader admin staff in Headquarters. We were, of course, very junior officers. All went well over the iced tomato soup until the Squadron Leader enquired what I had been doing at Helio airport. I told him about the dreaded Group Captain Horsley who had caught me not in the shelter – see previous story. I didn't paint a very nice picture of the CO and it was a few moments before realising that a heavy silence had descended over the table. There was more silence while I wondered what had gone wrong, when the mother said icily, "The Group Captain is a very dear friend of ours". There was further long silence followed by weak apology from me but too late to revive the happy atmosphere, and any chances with the daughter!

Then came orders for me to proceed to 239 Wing Training Flight at Darragh Main, a landing ground way out in the Tripolitanian desert to where, by then, the Jerries had been pushed back east. This meant getting a lift in whatever aircraft I could find going that way.

The Prime Minister, Winston Churchill, taking part in the
victory parade in Tripoli

51st Highland Division, complete with pipers, march through Tripoli

Western Desert coastline of North Africa from the DC3 Dakota

I found a Hudson pilot needing a 'second dickey' (second pilot) at Bilbeis landing ground near Cairo. He didn't seem to mind when I told him I had no experience flying twin-engine aircraft. The hot but pleasant flight to 'Marble Arch' (Arco Philaenorum - built by Mussolini) took just over five hours. It was the first time I had ever been to the toilet in an aeroplane. We let 'George'(autopilot) fly while we played cards. I persuaded an American to give me a lift in his DC-3 Dakota to Castle Benito in Tripolitania – just as a passenger this time. Then I went as passenger in another Hudson to Darragh Main. This was an area of desert scrubland cleared and surrounded by some empty 40-gallon (181 ltrs) drums and a few tents, to mark it out from the rest of the desert. I was getting near the enemy now.

This was the last training stage before being sent up against the enemy. Here I was taught those techniques of strafing and bombing, formations and disciplines of dog-fighting, etc, as used by the five squadrons of Kittyhawks of which 239 Wing comprised. I spent two weeks intensive Kittyhawk flying; twenty-one hours in the air.

The Flight Lieutenant commanding this flight called me into his tent to tell me that the Spitfire Wing Training Flight CO, not so far away, had been asking him where was this bloke Horden who was supposed to be on Spits? The Flight Lieutenant said that I had been sent to him in error. Having been trained on 'Hurries', I should now be on Spits! He gave me a choice: to stay or be transferred. I felt used to the Kittyhawk, was among good friends and so decided to stay. It was a difficult decision though – almost everyone wanted to be a glamorous Spitfire Pilot.

The other curious thing was that we were not to do front wheel landings! No, that was very cissy. Everyone here was proud to do accurate 3-point landings which, when properly carried out, would not cause ground loops. I remembered I had been on a special course of several hours' flying just to learn front-wheel landings – ah, well!

I learnt that the formation to be flown was twelve 'Kittys' in two boxes of six with the second box flying a few hundred feet above, behind and slightly to one side of the first six, preferably between them and the sun. (See the diagram on page 53.) Dive- bombing was from about 6,000–8,000 ft down to 1,000 ft (1828-2438 down to 304 m). The target was approached until it disappeared under the centre of the port wing, count to three and then go into a dive down to the left until the target was in front of the aircraft nose. At about 2,000 ft (609 m) pull up, count one, two and then release the bomb or bombs. Then we were to reform at about 5,000 ft (1524 m) in the same formation back to base. The dive was at about sixty degrees but felt like ninety!

Strafing was, of course, from low level. We followed each other down onto the target or targets. Sometimes dive-bombing would be followed immediately by strafing at ground level before reforming. The sky is a big place and often after bombing and strafing it was difficult to find other aircraft of any sort, the sky looked so empty, never mind a whole squadron to formate with. There will be more of this later when the action comes.

A sandstorm brewing up at 239 Wing Training Flight,
Darragh, Western Desert

Now it was decided that I should go to the famous 'Shark' Squadron, officially known as 112 Squadron to be pronounced "One-One-Two" squadron and definitely not "a hundred and twelve". Each Kittyhawk had a shark's mouth painted on the radiator under the nose and looked very menacing.

Johnnie Burcham was to go to 112 also and good friends Len Cherry and Eddie Ross, who had been with me at OTU in the Sudan, were joining the 'Sharks' too.

On 10 March 1943 we heard bad news from the Shark Squadron. Seven of the twelve Kittys had been shot down by a squadron of Me 109s diving on them in a surprise attack out of the sun. Only two of the 109s had been shot down in return. One of our pilots had baled out and got back to the squadron. Later we heard that two of ours were POWs so the other four died in the attack. A black day indeed for the Shark Squadron (see note 1 at the end of the chapter).

There were usually only about eighteen pilots on the Shark Squadron at any one time so they weren't called on for every operation. It was not surprising then that seven of us were moved up to the squadron as replacements, the very next day. The squadron was at another patch of desert, this time called Neffetia.

On 10 March, 112 had its blackest day as already described. In their dogfight and general melee, one of the Kittyhawk pilots, Flying Officer Ray 'Goose' Guess, also from Canada, shot down two 109Gs and one of these must have been Heinz Ludemann. This time Ludemann was killed. Unfortunately 'Western Desert Brown' was killed later by flak while dive-bombing enemy positions. 'Goose' Guess was shot down while flying over the Mount Etna region in Sicily and became a POW. I never did find out why he was called 'Goose' and we have now lost touch.

SHARK SQUADRON 1943 Full Formation

RED SECTION
No 1   +   +   +
No2   +   +   +
Green Red Yellow

BLUE SECTION
No 1   +   +   +
No 2   +   +   +
White Blue Black

RED ONE was also called 'LUDO' LEADER, 'Ludo' being the squadron call sign.

So what a pity those two pilots of the Shark squadron, who both shot down Heinz Ludemann, were not around to see the 109G take to the air again after 50 years. Myself and my wife Christine were at Duxford to see it arrive.

Note 1: One of our pilots shot down that day and who was taken prisoner, later died tragically. He took part in the Great Escape from Stalag Luft III in Poland. He was recaptured but was one of the fifty rounded up and shot on Hitler's order: Flying Officer George Wylie.

Note 2: In 1991 a ten year restoration to flying condition was completed at RAF Benson by Russ Snaddon and his team. In August 1991 it was flown to the Imperial War Museum site at Duxford to begin its career as a display aircraft (see Epilogue).

British and German squadron records and pilot's diaries show that this 109G was damaged in a dog-fight by Flight Sergeant W D Brown, a Canadian of 112 Squadron near Gambut, Cyrenaica (now Libya) in the Western Desert in 1942. The German pilot was Leutnant Heinz Ludemann who, although wounded, managed to force land in the desert. Ludemann got back to his squadron to fly again but the 109G was captured by the advancing 8th Army and, after evaluation, subsequently found its way back to the UK. There were two Browns on 112 squadron at the time and this one, for obvious reasons, was called 'Western Desert Brown'.

CHAPTER SEVEN

THE GOOLIE CHIT AND FIRST DOG-FIGHT

At 112 Squadron there was one mess for the pilots, of whatever rank, and all officers. It consisted of two EPIP tents; one as a lounge-bar and the other with tables for meals. The CO was the well-liked and respected Squadron Leader Geoff Garton who had won a DFC on Hurricanes in the Battle of Britain. He was fairly easy going on the ground but would not tolerate poor performance in the air. I learned that NCO pilots could be just as good as officers and, in fact, often a Flight Sergeant would lead the whole squadron of twelve Kittys into battle. Always in the corner of the mess tent was the 'gaggle board' showing the position each pilot was to fly in the formation for the next op. If one was on an early op the next day, Geoff Garton watched carefully that that pilot should stay off alcohol (if any available) and get to his sleeping tent in good time.

I was shortly to be on my first op, so had to learn a few things fast. I learned that navigation over the desert was not easy and there was a great incentive to avoid running out of petrol and having to force land. The Arabs did not like us and had a nasty tendency to cut off aircrew testicles, sew them up with camel hair thread in their mouths and set them loose in the desert. The one or two who survived this unfair treatment were most unhappy about it. So I was issued with a 'goolie-chit' to produce to Arabs, if necessary, offering large sums of money from the British Government, for returning aircrew unharmed.

The next important thing to learn was to wear long light khaki trousers and a long-sleeved shirt when flying, despite the heat. One of the pilots on 112, Jock Livingstone, was living proof of the validity of this advice. On a previous squadron flying Hurricanes on ops in Syria he had flown in shorts and short-sleeved shirt. His aircraft had been shot and burst into flames. Jock had to bale out but not before his skin, everywhere not covered, had been badly burnt. He was happy to show us the dreadful scars. Fortunately he had been wearing goggles so his eyes had been protected.

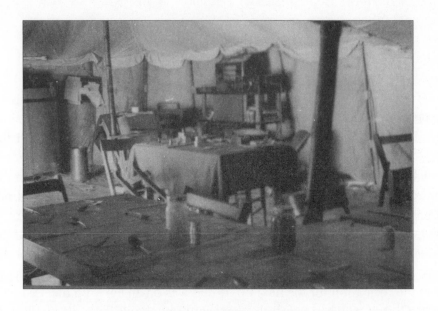

Shark Squadron pilots' Mess Tent, Tripolitania

That first night on my camp bed, I thought over what I had learned about the goolie-chits, the long trousers and the fact that the squadron had lost six pilots in a day. I felt a bit nervous as to what was in store but remembered how cheerful everyone was in the mess. Eventually, I dropped off to sleep.

Came the light of day and I was allocated to Kittyhawk 'Z' to share with another pilot. The squadron letters were GA painted on the side of the fuselage together with an individual letter: GA-Z. I usually flew this aircraft.

Most of us needed to have a nervous pee up against the tail wheel before take-off. Later a note appeared in DROs (Daily Routine Orders) telling us not to do this as it 'tends to corrode the rubber tyres which are becoming in short supply'!

There was a fitter and rigger, known as 'Erks' allocated to each aircraft. Z's fitter was 'Nick' Nicholas and he worked with me throughout my time on 112. One of them would sit on the wing to signal a safe taxying route to take-off point because the nose of the Kitty on the ground obstructed the pilot's view.

Then came the day I had been trained for all these months – my first operational flight. Because of the mini sandstorm we created at take-off, the whole squadron of twelve Kittys took off in formation, wing tip inside wing tip. Sometimes the resulting 'sandstorm' hung over the landing ground for half an hour or so.

As was the custom, I was to fly as 'number two' to Geoff Garton on my first trip. This necessitated 'weaving', pressing the rudder pedals to swing the tail from side to side, continually searching the sky for the enemy, to protect the 'number one' while he led the squadron. I was therefore the second aircraft off the ground with orders to stick with the CO like "shit to a blanket" to protect his tail whatever happened.

The Intelligence Officer briefed us first. This trip was a 'fighter' op to fly top cover to a squadron of Baltimore bombers, which were to attack enemy troop positions on the Mareth Line being tenaciously held by the Jerries. So we carried no bombs, just ammo trays in the wings, full of .5 inch (12.7 mm) bullets. There were three machine guns in each wing.

So we climbed into an open 13-cwt truck (cwt - hundredweight - a twentieth of an imperial ton), which delivered us to our respective aircraft around the dispersal area. I was flying 'Z' this time. I had my nervous pee and climbed in with parachute and Mae West (life jacket). Nick sat on the wing. I started up and taxied out for the formation take-off. I tucked my wing inside the CO's and off we went in a cloud of sand and dust. We climbed up, got into battle formation, found the Baltimores, got above them, between them and the sun, and off we set towards the enemy.

The slight twitching in my stomach disappeared as I concentrated on being a good number two to the CO. I searched the sky for Jerries but on this trip there were no enemy fighters to be seen. At this time of the

An armourer loading the ammunition trays for the six .5 (12.7mm) machine guns

The 'business end' of a Kittyhawk

desert war we had almost gained complete air-superiority. The sun beat on the cockpit hood as we flew along with the Allison engines roaring steadily. The Baltimores seemed to move slowly below us over the almost featureless desert.

About half an hour after take-off things began to happen. Big black silent puffs appeared among the bombers. This was anti-aircraft fire from German 88mm guns that were highly accurate either as ack-ack or against tanks and other targets at ground level. The Allies had nothing quite like it. I soon learnt that this ack-ack was a killer.

On the ground there erupted clouds of dust among German Afrika Korps emplacements as the Baltimores dropped their bombs on and around the target. Then the black puffs began to burst among us. Could hear a faint crump-crump over the engine noise. The CO changed course to put off the German gunners and the whole squadron followed with the top flight keeping as much up-sun as possible. Being shot at was to become almost a daily occurrence but I never quite got over the feeling that someone was trying to kill me, having always wanted to be loved!

The CO set course for base together with the bombers. We came in to land amid the dust, in echelon starboard, in two flights of six, the second flight having to cope with the usual mini sandstorm. There were no aircraft losses at all, that trip. Nick was there to guide me taxying to the right dispersal point. It was a wonderful feeling of exhilaration and confidence having survived the first op. I was in the air one hour twenty minutes. I felt more at ease in the pilots mess that night having been blooded.

The squadron crest consisted of the usual circle with crown above but with an Egyptian Cat in the middle. Under were the words 'Swift in Destruction'. The original artwork, signed by King George VI and framed, was kept in the mess tent. One-One-Two had been a night-fighter squadron with Sopwith Camels in WWI, reformed for WWII.

The distinctive shark's mouth had been painted on one of the first Tomahawks, flown earlier, by Flying Officer Westernra and was so spectacular it had been taken up as a semi-official insignia for all 112 Squadron aircraft, thereby originating the idea, later copied by the American Flying Tigers in China and many others over the years. Some of us wanted to change the cat for a shark on the crest but higher authority would not hear of it. It would mean approaching the King for his agreement!

One-One-Two Squadron crest signed by King George VI

No 239 Wing consisted of five Kittyhawk squadrons: 250 Sqn RAF, 260 Sqn RAF, 3 Sqn RAAF, 450 Sqn RAF and 112 Sqn RAF. On 112 Sqn there were pilots from all over the Empire: South Africans, Canadians, Rhodesians, Australians, Kenyans and New Zealanders as well as Irishmen, Welshmen, Scots and Englishmen plus at least one American.

The Intelligence Officer (IO) worked mainly in the shade of a 3-ton truck and organized a large map covering our operational area and showing the 'bomb-line'. This line was, as near as possible, the army's front line. Certainly no bombs were to be dropped on our side of this line as they could drop on our own troops. It was adjusted daily by the IO in cooperation with the 8th Army. At this time the Germans had dug in along the Mareth Line and that was where most of the action took place.

On 22nd March we were off again on my second op. This time we carried two 250lb bombs on a special rack under the belly of the aircraft and our job was to dive-bomb and strafe enemy positions. All went well until we got over the Germans, then up came those black puffs of 88mm ack-ack. Continual changes of course were necessary to try and upset the gunners' aim. Again this was successful for we could see black puffs where we would have been if we hadn't altered course.

The 2 x 250lb bomb rack that earned an MBE for its inventor

All of us, especially the No 2s, were on the lookout for enemy aircraft, especially up in the sun and could press the R/T transmit button on the throttle to give a warning to the leader and indeed all of us. At other times we were to keep radio silence. This time someone shouted 'Bandits at 2 o'clock above!' Sure enough four Me 109s came screaming down upon us out of the sun.

Our instructions were not to risk our aircraft in dog-fights with German fighters, but, needless to say, we all wanted to have a go and the order was not always obeyed. My job was to stick with my No 1 as his rear protection and at the same time avoid enemy fire.

The Squadron turned in towards the diving Me 109s but began to lose formation as we all tried to get on the tail of the enemy. The leader called up on the R/T to jettison bombs which we did, hopefully, the other side of the bomb-line. I had a second's glimpse of a 109 with its yellow propeller spinner and tracers zipping past the top of my cockpit. I tried desperately to get on his tail but he was away. Presume they also had orders to have one surprise attack at the twelve Kittyhawks and then escape to fight another day, which is what they did.

Suddenly the sky was empty. I had been wondering how I would cope with such a situation. A lone Kittyhawk was an easy target for any more 109s that may be around. I lost a bit of height to see more sky. After a few sweating moments I saw some aircraft above and away south, so I opened up the throttle and eventually caught up with the reforming squadron on its way back to base, weaving all the way to ensure no enemy was on my tail. A bit of luck and much relief.

Although the operation had to be aborted, again we suffered no losses. One Kitty had bullet holes. I thought I might have been reprimanded for getting separated from my No 1 but, as the same thing had happened to all the No 2s, nothing was said. I had survived my first air-to-air combat.

CHAPTER EIGHT

THE EXHILARATION OF STRAFING

We all felt something big was happening this day. First, all pilots were to attend the IO (Intelligence Officer) who explained that the New Zealand Division of the 8th Army had been secretly moved to a position on the left flank to begin what was hoped to be the final squeeze and push to clear the Jerries out of North Africa. They had removed their uniform buttons and badges and had moved by truck, a few at a time, to ensure the enemy was unaware. The local Arab spies would supply information to anyone who would pay. There was just beginning a mighty battle and we were to assist the New Zealanders on their push forward up the main road through a valley to El Hamma, with bombing and strafing support.

So our Kittys were each armed with two 250 lb (113 kg) bombs under their fuselages. Twelve-inch rods were attached to the nose cones of the bombs so they would explode just above the ground. We also carried six 40 lb (18 kg) anti-personnel bombs under the wings.

Before going we were to attend a Wing pep talk by Group Captain Harry Broadhurst from Group Headquarters. There must have been nearly eighty pilots gathered around the Group Captain as he stood in the back of a 3-ton truck to deliver his oration. Shades of Agincourt! He was most depressing. He told us we were an important factor in this great battle just beginning. He said that some of us would have to walk back, some would be prisoners of war and some of us would not get back at all! But, of course, he knew he could count on us all to do our duty, etc, etc. I was not motivated – just plain shit scared.

*Shark 'Kitty' with unique bomb-rack carrying two 250lb (113 kilo)
bombs fitted with anti-personnel nose rods*

*In this view the extended rods in the nose of the bombs, designed to
make them burst at or above ground level, can be clearly seen*

Back at the squadron I learned that I was to fly No 2 to the CO again. I felt better about this because he inspired confidence. He told me to stick as close to him as possible all the way from a formation take-off to, hopefully, a formation landing on our return. So the squadron took off, CO first followed by myself, tucked in as tight as I dare, then the other ten Kittys (the jacket illustration was chosen because it could so easily have been the CO and myself taking off).

Our work was close army support so our base was always close up behind the Army. When they moved forward, so did we. So it was not many minutes flying to our target area. On the way we could see other Kittyhawk squadrons moving towards the same area. It was all very well having a clear bomb-line on a map in the IO's truck but there was little on the ground to indicate where our lot ended and the Jerries began. This time, however, along the main road up the valley to El Hamma we could see tanks and trucks moving up, while beyond, in enemy held territory there was little to see.

Geoff Garton soon identified some German 88 mm gun emplacements for us to bomb. There was no ack-ack aimed at us at this stage as no doubt the German gunners were pointing their guns up the road at the New Zealanders' tanks instead of at us. The CO went down. Then it was my turn. I clearly saw the emplacements disappear under my port wing before going down to the left. The dive felt like 90 degrees but was only about 60. I saw the CO's bombs burst on target just as I released mine. Others that followed also found the target so it was good accurate bombing. It wasn't always.

Now we were to strafe any enemy targets that we could find. I saw some other guns at the side of the road and set about strafing. The six .5 inch guns (12.7 mm) all firing could be felt as a braking sensation on the flight of the Kitty and the destructive power at the receiving end was enormous. Most were explosive bullets mixed with a few tracers. As I went in to strafe, I noticed some objects shooting past the cockpit hood. At first I thought we were being attacked by enemy fighters but they were large objects. Then realized they were artillery shells the New Zealanders were lobbing at the enemy – or vice versa – I didn't stop to find out which.

I continued strafing for a short time with tracers going into the enemy positions. Some small arms fire came up at me. Then I pulled up to orientate myself, only to find I was completely on my own again; not an aircraft in sight. I spotted some German trucks scurrying at high speed down the road – a rare sight – so set about them. I caught the rear truck, which burst into flames. I saw my bullets spraying the other two which crashed off the road into the scrub but didn't flame. I couldn't see any more targets and thought I may be nearly out of ammunition so pulled up and set off towards base. I wondered what the CO would say when we got back. I was half way when I spotted a lone aircraft at about 5,000 ft (1524 m). I gradually caught up with it, made sure it was one of ours and, to my amazement, it was the CO. What luck! He waved to me. I think he was as amazed as I was, so I tucked in behind him to guard his tail and shortly arrived over base. I did a very close formation landing in the hopes of impressing him. At the de-briefing he nodded his thanks for staying with him.

After all Harry Broadhurst's doom and gloom the whole wing lost only one Kittyhawk. I didn't see it myself but apparently it had crashed into the hillside past the target area. It could have been pilot's error for there was little ack-ack, in fact less than on most of our ops.

For our attack on the El Hamma battle area, the Wing received a signal from Monty to say thank-you for good work. Monty was thoughtful like that. Sometimes an individual squadron received a signal from him showing that he had gone to the trouble to find out exactly who had done the good job.

The prominent feature of desert life in Tripolitania (now Libya) was the heat during each day. The sun shone remorselessly down upon us. The only shelter from the direct sun was in a tent and that could be very hot. Like everything else we got used to it. It had its advantages too. When we had enough water to wash ourselves we didn't need a towel – we were dry in a few moments! It was a good clean dry heat. No one had colds in the desert – no germs lived there. An egg would fry nicely on a hot stone in the desert sunlight. The 'Desert Rats' of the 8th Army used to fry eggs – when available – on the flat parts of their tanks – a common sight in the desert. However, it could be bitterly cold at night and we learned to have the same number of layers of blanket under as well as over us on our canvas camp beds. There was gritty sand everywhere, even in the food. It was no use trying to avoid it – just get used to it.

For food we had mostly hard tack – such as ship's biscuits – with a little tinned butter, which tasted rancid, and Spam or bully beef. Our camp cook bragged that he could cook Spam in thirty different ways. Bully beef we called 'desert chicken' in memory of eating a real chicken if we ever came across such a luxury. We did get the luxury of an occasional chicken's egg by bartering some tea or bully beef with passing Arabs. "Eggies for chi?" was the opening question. Water was strictly rationed as it all had to be brought to us from a distance in small tankers pulled behind lorries. Usually the ration was one personal water bottle per day. That was for washing and shaving. Morale demanded that we shave every day. In addition we got two or three enamel mugs of tea from the cookhouse tent. Strangely we seemed to have more petrol than water so we resorted to washing our clothes in it. It was a bit smelly till it evaporated in the hot sun but was definitely better than wearing sweat-stained clothes.

In the mess tent we had a radio to listen to the BBC Overseas Service or Lord Haw-Haw from Germany. We liked him because we could laugh at his propaganda and he played our favourite record – Lillie Marlene. Of course we listened to our own Vera Lynn and the favourite dance bands of the time. We even had a gramophone with some Glen Miller and other records. A pilot of 260 Squadron was shot down in the desert behind enemy lines and walked his way back. He spotted a German camp ahead and couldn't see any way round it, so lay down till dark when he hoped to bluff his way through. He couldn't think of any German words so boldly walked unnoticed right through the middle of the camp loudly whistling Lillie Marlene! He got back safely.

We had a captured Savoia–Marchetti 81, three-engined Italian bomber and when we could get it to go, which was not often, sent someone on a trip back to the Delta for some booze and cigarettes. The drink was only a few cans of American beer and a few ghastly 'V' cigarettes made in India. There was a rare ration of Players cigarettes in round tins of fifty. Fitter Nick didn't smoke so I used to trade with him some beer from our mess.

We kept fit and sun burnt, nearly as brown as the Arabs. Strange as it may seem, many of us had become very fond of the clean life, way out in the desert away from civilization.

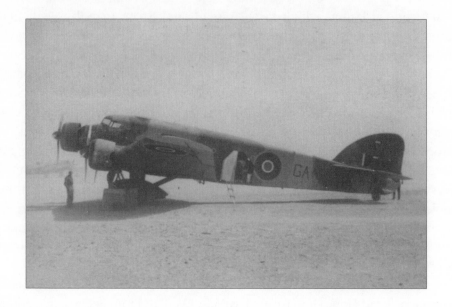

A captured Savoia Marchetti SM81, the transport for the Squadron.
We never did get it to run on more than two engines at a time

CHAPTER NINE

HORRORS OF WAR

The Jerries were gradually being pushed further and further back. Soon there would be little left of North Africa held by them. The trouble was that all the ack-ack guns were moving with them so it got more and more concentrated. The coast road between Gabes and Sfax in Tunisia was heavily defended. Our job on 28 March was to destroy as much as possible of Jerry transport moving along that road or hidden nearby. Again we carried two 250lb bombs under the fuselage as well as the 40-pounders under the wings. At first it seemed easy. As we prepared to bomb there were no black puffs of 88 mm. However, as we dived down over the target there was very intense light ack-ack at 1,000ft – 2,000ft (304 - 609 m) probably from Breda guns. Tracers were coming up from all directions. There was no way to avoid it, just continue with the dive and trust to luck. As I pulled out of the dive I saw one Kittyhawk on fire. It just continued down instead of pulling out of the dive and went straight into the ground with a burst of flame and black smoke. There was no parachute, no chance of living through that. I didn't know who it was till we got back to base. Fortunately the leader had the sense to abandon any strafing run now that the Jerries were all prepared for us – so we went back home. At de-briefing I discovered that it was a South African pilot we had lost. He had only joined us a few days before.

Next morning we went to a similar target. This time we saw a German encampment near the road and bombed that. The top flight bombed more MT on the road. Again the ack-ack was intense but all returned safely. In the afternoon we went up again, this time to find a small German vessel reported to be escaping from a harbour north of Gabes. I remembered we had nose-rods on our bombs. We didn't have time to change them for more suitable types for anti-shipping. We flew over the blue Med for a few minutes at about 6,000 ft (1828 m) and, sure enough, there was a boat. Could it be a German E-boat, we wondered, heading out to sea at high speed? We got into bombing position. I was fourth down this time. Our bombs dropped into the sea all around the vessel. I thought I had got a direct hit but wasn't sure. We came back to base within forty-five minutes.

A result of our dive bombing. A German PzKpfw II
(Panzerkampfwagen Mk II) Ausf F

More bomb damage attributed to One-One-Two

At de-briefing I was congratulated by everyone on my direct hit. An hour or so later the IO brought us terrible news. The boat we had bombed was an RAF Air-Sea Rescue Boat. The one bomb that hit, having a nose rod, did not sink the boat but shrapnel from it had killed a crewman on deck. There had been a terrible communications mix-up and our leader had seen no identification signs to show it was one of ours. It was no one's fault – just one of the dreadful things that happen in wartime. We knew that worse things could befall millions if the Jerries were not to be defeated.

When the Court of Inquiry was eventually convened, the CO told me, thoughtlessly I felt, that I had better be the one to attend. I waited for hours at the Court tent only to be told that the Inquiry had been postponed for lack of witnesses. I told the CO that, whether it was reconvened or not, I didn't want to go through the ordeal. Fortunately he agreed. I never did hear who got blamed for the mix-up. I felt dreadful about it – beyond words – but just had to press on with my tour of ops and try to put it to the back of my mind – but, of course, I can never forget.

The squadron moved up close behind our army front lines to give them support as they slowly but surely pushed the Jerries, and what was left of the Italians, out of Tunisia and North Africa, in April 1943. The New Zealanders had cleared an area for landing and take-offs at El Hamma and for a few hours we operated from there. That evening Jerry shells began to explode on the edge of this landing ground and we were advised to dig in.

Despite a shortage of spades, we dug holes inside our tents so that we could lie down on our camp beds just below the surface of the ground to avoid flying shrapnel. Still the Jerries kept lobbing the occasional shell among us. We took a poor view of this – most unfair. We expected to be shot at in the air but being shot at on the ground as well was a bit much.

Our Kittyhawks were dispersed at the far side of the area out of harm's way, as we first thought. The Jerry gunners were on the side of a hill overlooking our movements and began to get ambitious regarding our aeroplanes. They brought their infamous 88 mm guns that were as good firing at ground targets as they were at aircraft and on the following morning at first light began a heavy shelling.

Still determined to shave every morning regardless of all problems, I was trying to use my razor while lying down on my camp bed below ground, when the shelling got worse and shrapnel zipped through the tent above me. I was glad when the order came to evacuate ourselves and the Kittys to somewhere safer. We ran out to our aircraft and took off individually, as fast as possible all willy-nilly instead of in our usual tidy formation.

I took off in my 'Z' amid shellfire and shell holes. I could see shells exploding as my wheels left the ground. For once I felt safer in the air than on the ground. We had to leave one Kitty behind as it became damaged from shell-fire but we got it back later, after a South African squadron found the Jerry gun emplacements and destroyed them. In the meantime we operated from a landing ground named Medenine Main.

As the Jerries retreated they were most uncooperative in that they ploughed up their landing grounds with a tractor before they left, so we had to keep clearing our own landing areas. One day I caught a tractor actually at work, ploughing round and round in ever increasing circles. I went down to take a pot shot at it. As I did the driver abandoned his tractor and ran off. I concentrated on the tractor, which burst into flames. How many Jerry tractors does one have to shoot down to become an ace, I wondered? I often thought about the driver. Was he an Arab forced to do this dangerous job? Or was he a German soldier? I shall never know.

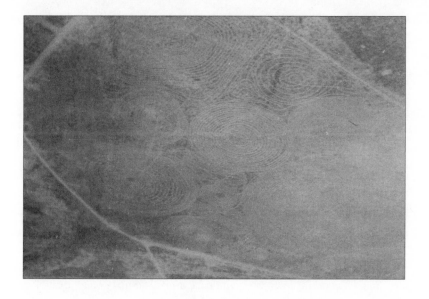

A former German occupied landing ground, completely ploughed up before they left to render it useless for Allied operations

It was about this time that we pitched our tents among abandoned Jerry artillery equipment, the most interesting being a plentiful supply of cordite sticks. This remarkable stuff burns without oxygen and is fun to bury underground with one stick protruding. Light this and there is a miniature volcanic eruption. We progressed to filling empty potato tins with the cordite, hammering together the open end to form a jet. Not quite up to Frank Whittle standard but they did make wonderful rockets rising to a few hundred feet. Higher authority thought we might shoot down one of our own Kittyhawks so we had to abandon this rather juvenile activity.

In mid April the weather deteriorated with high Kamsin winds and a lot of sand blowing up. One day we tried to carry out an armed reconnaissance but had to turn back before getting to the bomb-line. It was not much fun landing in a sandstorm and it didn't count as an op.

Shark Squadron Kittyhawk with 63 gallon (286 litre) belly tank.
Western Desert August, 1943

Sometimes 112 would fly as top fighter cover to another Kitty squadron. The P-40 Kittyhawk was no match for the Jerry Me 109s so it was fortunate we had mainly air superiority and didn't often have to dogfight with the enemy. About this time the relatively new Focke-Wulf 190 appeared in the sky over North Africa. We had heard how lethal they were. One day 112 acted as fighter top cover to 260 Kittyhawk Squadron. We carried no bombs or long-range belly tanks so we were ready to meet any fighter opposition – we thought. It was a lovely fine sunny day and most pleasant flying along in formation way above 260 who had all the unpleasant work to do. Sure enough the flak started to burst among 260's Kittys as they arrived over the target. Sadly one burst into flames and went down and the pilot was obviously killed.

When I saw this I had a curious feeling of elation. I couldn't understand it and for some time I felt ashamed of this reaction. Later, on talking with other pilots, I found it was a natural reaction to be glad it wasn't oneself that got shot. I understood that all men in action felt this way, so I gave up worrying.

As we headed for home there were some four enemy fighters coming down upon us out of the sun. As they screamed down they opened fire for a short burst, scattering our formation all over the sky. One of them passed me at high speed in a dive and I recognized it clearly as a Fw 190, the first I had seen. After all that commotion and heart skipping a few beats, we re-formed without loss and escorted 260 Squadron back to base.

Pilots and Officers of Shark Squadron, March 1943. The Commanding Officer, Geoff Garton DFC, is seated front centre. 'Taffy' Evans the Adjutant is looking over his right shoulder

On another armed recce near Sfax we found a whole road full of enemy transport and tanks, quite a rare sight. Jerry did most of his moving around at night. I went down to bomb. There was so little enemy fire, only small arms, so I thought it worth risking a strafing run. It was very exciting shooting up Jerry transport. Our tracers helped us get the .5 inch bullets on target. Our firepower from the six guns was devastating and often motor transport burst into satisfying flames. On this trip I personally got three trucks burning and the other pilots got many more between them. I didn't stay around long enough to get caught by the Jerries bringing their ack-ack guns into play. We were all back safe and sound this time too, but Nick found several bullet holes in the fuselage of my 'Z'.

CHAPTER TEN

VICTORY IN NORTH AFRICA

The town of Tunis fell to us. The Germans had their backs to the Med. What was left of their army was all concentrated in the Cap Bon peninsular. Their defeat in North Africa was certain and imminent. Their one objective was to withdraw to Sicily with as much of their personnel and equipment as they could save. What was left of the Italian Army and Regia Aeronautica was much despised by both sides as to their fighting qualities but, to be fair, their heart was just not in it. The result was that the Eyeties mostly got left behind by the Jerries.

The Germans had, of course, only two ways to escape: in the air or by ship. Therefore our objective was to prevent both. We carried out many fighter sweeps over the sea north of Cap Bon. On 18 April we set off looking for escaping Ju 52s full of troops. We patrolled for some time but the Jerries were probably waiting for nightfall. We were just about to turn back towards base when up came the flak from Cap Bon. There was a big explosion around my 'Z' and the engine started to vibrate frighteningly. I had the feeling this could be the end of my tour but again I was lucky. I called up the leader to explain and he deputed Sergeant Hounsell to escort me back to base or at least see what happened to me. Fortunately there was no further flak. I landed all right to find large chunks of 88mm shrapnel in one wing and some small chunks out of the propeller. Nick changed the prop and my rigger patched up the holes in the wing. I tested the engine which seemed all right so I flew it again twice the next day on more fighter sweeps. I saw some Me 109s again but they cleared off smartly when they saw our formation. I don't think for a moment that they were scared, just prudent, for there were many Allied aircraft in the air for one of theirs most of the time.

Two days later we were doing the same sort of work off Cap Bon when we ran into heavy ack-ack followed by being jumped on by a whole squadron of Me 109s. There was a terrific mêlée. I tried desperately to get on the tail of a Me 109 and did get to fire guns but my tracer fell behind him as he turned tightly. I saw two of our Kittyhawks on fire and one pilot bale out. Then suddenly the sky was empty. I found some Kittys on the way back and got into some sort of formation in time to descend towards base. At de-briefing I found that we had lost three sergeant pilots: Prain, Hounsell (who had helped me but three days before) and Lamont. Their bodies were never found. Our pilots claimed two Me 109s damaged but no one could confirm their destruction.

The next day our target was an enemy troopship ten miles out over the sea from Cap Bon. We couldn't find it but I noticed how surprising it was that the engine always sounded rough as we got out of sight of land! Instead of a ship we found a Me 110 flying just under a cloud base at about 8,000 ft (2438 m). The whole squadron set after it like a pack of hounds after a fox. To our amazement it dived down towards the sea. If the pilot had pulled up into cloud he would have got away. Several of us got in shots at him and he developed a fire in the cockpit. He went lower and lower until his wing-tip touched the water. Then he crashed into the sea while one of his crew fired off Verey Lights, or the German equivalent, hopefully to get a rescue from Cap Bon, a few miles away. We came away and left them to it as they climbed into their life-raft. I claimed one seventh of a Me 110! We were two hours in the air, a little longer than most of our ops at that time.

I learned another useful lesson: never fly close behind another Kitty when he is firing his guns. From his guns are released all the empty shells and they could easily puncture one's radiator and lose the glycol coolant. I got away with it this time.

Three days later we set off again to find a Jerry troopship off Cap Bon. We found it this time and dive-bombed among some light ack-ack. Our bombs fell all around it, some close along side but we couldn't be sure of success. The next day the Navy informed us they could confirm that we had sunk it.

On 1 May we were sent out on another anti-shipping patrol with just one 500 lb (226 kg) bomb each and saw no ships, so we thought we would bomb some warehouses on a quayside. Several of us got direct hits this time. The warehouse must have been full of explosives for it blew up in a tremendous fireball with smoke rising to 1,000 ft (304 m) or more. It was very satisfying. On the way back we were attacked by two 109s but they made only one pass at us and then cleared off. We all came back safely.

We had a marvellous 'Y' Service beavering away for us. Linguists with radios monitored all they could hear of German broadcasts and messages. Each little snippet of knowledge gained was fitted into a picture like a jigsaw until really useful information resulted. One excellent example was as the Germans were evacuating Cap Bon. They had assembled, under careful camouflage, several huge 6-engined aircraft called Me 323s. Each could carry 200 troops at a time.

A burnt out Me 323, six engine troop transport.
Elouina Airport, Tunis, May 1943

Our 'Y' Service gleaned that they were to take off fully laden with retreating crack troops on a certain day early in May. As the 'Y' Service couldn't find the exact time, several Kittyhawk squadrons were to patrol off Cap Bon at different times in the hope of catching them. 112 was the fourth squadron to arrive on the scene. As we approached we learned that a South African squadron had been successful just before us. The scene, when we arrived, was almost unbelievable. Three of these huge Me 323s were sinking into the sea and hundreds of Jerry troops were swimming around in the water. The South Africans told us later that they had intercepted these aircraft just after take-off from Cap Bon. They were almost sitting targets, just wallowing through the air, each heavily laden with troops and the six engines struggling to maintain height. The only defensive action was as the troops inside poked their rifles out of the windows of the 323s and shot at the Kittyhawks with little effect. On this trip there was nothing to do but return to report the South Africans' success and wonder what happened to the unfortunate Germans.

The German army could no longer cope and large numbers of them and many Eyeties (Italians) just hung around awaiting directions to our prison camps. These 'prison camps' were merely areas set aside in fields where perhaps, eventually, our people would give them some food and water.

A 'do it yourself' prisoner of war camp for both Germans and Italians.
Cap Bon, Tunisia, May 1943

Those of us not flying took a truck and set off to see these sights. German and Italian officers seemed to like to give themselves up to RAF pilots and willingly handed us their Luger or Beretta handguns. Some of them drove themselves towards these camps in all sorts of vehicles. This meant that most of us pilots returned to the squadron base in our own transport, ranging from Auto-Union jeep type vehicles to saloon cars and, of course, all carrying a captured hand gun.

A captured Auto Union general utility. Pressed into service as the
Pilots' transport. Zuara, May 1943

This was where I made a mistake. Thinking to be clever I hung around the POWs longer than the others until an Italian officer came to give himself up driving a lovely black Fiat saloon car. This was just what I had been waiting for. I showed the Eyetie into the camp and drove back to base in his car and with his Beretta hand gun. Everyone admired the car. It was definitely the best bit of war trophy on the squadron. When the CO saw it he explained that it was natural for the CO to have the best vehicle to drive around in – so promptly appropriated it!

We carried out several more armed recces over the Med looking for enemy shipping but largely it had been cleared up by the Royal Navy. One interesting trip was when the Navy captured the island of Pantelleria from the enemy. This island is between Cap Bon and Sicily and is too small to warrant a landing ground but was held by a few German and Italian troops.

The Royal Navy sent three destroyers to take the island and our job was to patrol over them in turns to protect them from air attacks. When our turn came, just Pilot Officer Reg Wild and myself, as No 2, set off for a two-hour stint. Within a few minutes we had located the destroyers, a wonderful sight steaming majestically towards the enemy. They should have been told we were to be there, and maybe they were, but they were taking no chances with their aircraft recognition. As we approached they put up a carpet of flak a few hundred feet below us. So we patrolled at a respectful distance, up sun, watching the destroyers approach the island, myself weaving from side to side across Reg's tail, looking everywhere for any sign of the enemy. I got a stiff neck looking around but was better than a bullet in the backside. In the event the Navy took Pantelleria without any resistance. There were no enemy aircraft that time either, so it was an easy trip for us and we returned without other incident.

The battle for North Africa was over. Now the squadron withdrew to Zuara, east along the coast, for a short period of training and relaxation. I had carried out twenty-eight operational sorties, being shot at most of the time and the CO said I was experienced enough to fly as No 1. So before we went back into battle I had several practice formation flights acting in this new position.

I had got so used to flying Kittyhawks that they began to feel like extensions to my body. I could fly close accurate formation when needed and could land within a few feet of where I wanted. It was a great feeling to return to base after a frightening trip, see the landing ground with squadron ambulance waiting just in case, side-slip off a few feet of height and make a good landing in front of the waiting and watching ground staff. Showing off no doubt as young men will.

Squadron Leader Geoff Garton DFC, our popular CO, was now 'tour expired' and went back to a post in Egypt. His place was taken by Squadron Leader George Norton, not so experienced in battle.

The Squadron ambulance

We were expecting a visit from a VIP. No one was yet prepared to say who it was. Several squadrons of Kittyhawks and other aircraft flew to Sawman – another larger landing ground on the coast. One Kitty made a bad landing and broke a leg of its undercarriage. So it sat in the middle of the landing ground in the way of other aircraft landing. The VIP was about to land in a large aircraft, so a tractor was sent to drag the broken Kitty quickly out of the way and hide it under the palm trees. We were shocked because this precipitate action made the damage to the Kitty much worse and we had quite rightly been trained to cosset our aircraft at all costs. So all was ready for the VIP and it was revealed to us that it was to be King George VI. His aircraft landed safely and we were honoured to be inspected and addressed by him with our Kittyhawks all lined up in a straight row – wing tip to wing tip. I personally loved the man and thought he epitomized all we were fighting for. I think most of us felt the same.

Then it was back to Zuara. I got a weekend in Alexandria allowed, so I went in a Hudson of 117 Squadron for this quick break. It was all very well but strangely I was glad to get back to friends and to get on with the war. I knew I had many ops to do to complete my tour.

All was very relaxed at Zuara. The only flying we did was not operational and there were no attacks from enemy bombers at that time. New pilots arrived from all over the Empire to replace those lost or tour expired. A new arrival would be surprised to hear various pilots discussing his weight! There was a lot of guessing and as the evening got nearer, bets were being placed. Was he over ten stone (63.5 kg) or nearer nine (57 kg)? Much argument broke out and the bewildered new arrival just couldn't make out what it was all about. When the bar had been open for a while and everyone was in a good mood the CO would say: "I'm fed up with all this argument, let's settle it once and for all".

The newcomer was asked to sit down on the sandy mess floor. One pilot sat behind him with his arms under the subject's armpits. Another pilot sat at his feet with his arms around them. Then by leaning backwards, the subject, much to his astonishment, would be levered off the ground. While he was in this position, not being able to do anything at all, someone would undo his fly-buttons and pour in a pint of beer. So this new pilot, of whatever rank, was fully blooded with our 'weight lifting' and ready to start flying as a No 2.

Taffy, the Adjutant, was a cheery little round-faced man somewhat older than we pilots and very, very proper indeed – an ex-schoolmaster. He was not a practical man at all, administrative only. The bawdy songs we sang of an evening, in the mess tent, embarrassed him greatly. He therefore became the butt of much teasing and some jokes. He tried to be strict regarding the way the erks dressed, despite the fact that they all plodded around in khaki shorts and little else in the African sun. One time he put my fitter Nick on a charge for not wearing his forage cap while working on my Kitty. When I explained to Taffy that these Kittyhawks were fitted with Mark II slipstreams which blew our hats off, he swallowed it hook, line and sinker.

On the beach at Zuara was a bungalow among the palm trees. It was inhabited by black girls and a big fat momma running as a brothel. There was great discussion whether it should be 'legalised' with the MO making a daily inspection, or whether it should be put 'out of bounds'. Our local 8th Army Newssheet reported that Lady Asquith in the House of

Commons was running a campaign against servicemen being allowed into brothels at all, never mind 'legalising' them. It was decided by the CO to put it out of bounds. Taffy the Adjutant, thought it his duty to make sure none of our airmen visited there, so he used to peer in the windows, much to our amusement (and probably his!). One day Taffy came running back to the CO to report that he had seen one of our erks actually 'on the job' and worse still, actually wearing his forage cap at the same time!

Eventually some coloured American Army GIs took over the bungalow. We moved on.

In the desert our Kittys had a problem of sand getting into the bearings causing engine failure. Each engine was fitted with a Kuno oil filter and before the bearings were likely to seize up, 'silver fish' would appear there. When these bits of bearing metal were found, then the Kitty had to have an engine change. It was the pilot's duty, together with his fitter, after every day's flying, to examine the Kuno air filter.

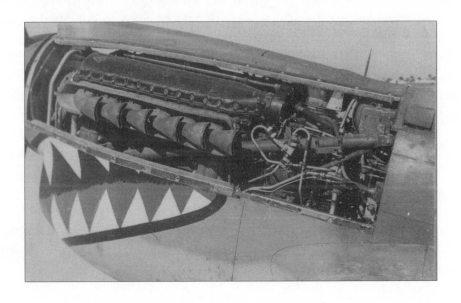

Allison F4R engine which powered the Kittyhawks. The Kuno desert air filter was mounted on the opposite side

Kittyhawks were made by Curtis in the States and early ones had Allison in-line engines. Other later marques had Packard Merlins, built by Packard in the States under licence from Rolls Royce.

We pilots were equipped with escaping and evading gadgets in the event that we were shot down the wrong side of the bomb-line. First I always flew with a .38 (approx 9 mm) revolver in its webbing holster around the waist, although I don't know who on earth I would shoot at. Anyway, I felt safer with it available. A clever article we carried was a propelling pencil with chrome pocket clip, which was magnetized. Slip off the clip and balance it on the point of the pencil and we had a compass. We all carried a slip of silk printed with a map of the area. It screwed up very small so was easy to hide about one's person.

We assumed, rightly, that we would be going on to invade Italy or somewhere into 'the soft underbelly of Europe' as the American commentators liked to say. The weather would be different and we were equipped with escape flying boots. They were beautifully made with an unmarked penknife tucked secretly inside which could be used to cut off the calf length of leather, leaving ordinary looking brown shoes. The calf lengths were fleece lined and could be tucked under the shirt around one's body to keep out the cold. I always flew in them but fortunately never did have to use them in anger, so to speak. Many of those shot down in enemy territory were extremely glad of them, we later heard.

The American armed forces began to appear in the area. Their Army Air Force, mostly bombers, had moved into Egypt to give us support and, of course, had invaded North Africa from the west to help squeeze out the Hun and what was left of the Eyeties. The Americans called the locals "Gen-oo-ine Bed-oo-ine A-rabs" and generally played havoc with the local economy by paying over the odds for everything. We told them to "get your knees brown", for they had no experience of desert warfare. However we were now poised to invade Europe.

CHAPTER ELEVEN

THE BODY IN THE DRINKING WATER

Now it was time to go back into action, 112 Squadron was to operate from an airfield in Malta to support the army on its invasion of Sicily. The squadron motor transport and ground staff went by sea from Tripoli. Some pilots including myself were taken in special commissioned DC3 Dakotas and shortly we all arrived on Safi airfield, Malta, to commence operations.

Valetta , Malta, harbouring many terribly damaged ships

Malta itself, especially Valetta, was mostly in ruins and the harbour was half full of stricken RN and other ships. The people were not in good health having endured terrible bombardments and shortages of proper food over the last few months. It was noticeable that the local population had many skin sores due to malnutrition. However that is another story; George Cross Island.

Next day we took off for close support to the army between Gerbini and Raddusa in Sicily. The road was busy with all sorts of German motor transport and the flak was very heavy even at 8,000 ft (2438 m). We dived through it all. Transport on the road and some hidden off the road was hit. As we went down in the dive much light ack-ack was thrown up. I didn't see the CO pull out of his dive but was busy trying to pull up before hitting the hillside myself. I could feel and hear some nasty sounding clangs as shells and shrapnel hit the fuselage of my 'Z'. I could see our bombs still landing among the transport. It wasn't the time or place to go back for a strafing run, so we straggled back to Malta.

At de-briefing we learned that the CO had been killed. Others had seen him hit by flak and crash into the ground. It was his first and last operational trip with the squadron.

On this trip my 'Z' had many holes, mostly in the fuselage but they were soon patched by my rigger. The Jerries still had many guns operating despite their defeat in North Africa. Reinforcements had come via Italy no doubt.

Dive-bombing caused some physical problems for the pilot. Starting perhaps at 6,000 – 8,000 ft (1828- 2438 m) and only starting to pull out at about 2,000 ft (609 m), meant a great force of gravity known simply as 'G', pushing us down into our seats and causing a blackout for a second or two as we came out of it. Also it was painful for the eardrums. Our squadron MO often told us, with a 'tut-tut', that we would suffer for it in later life. He was right of course. There was also the danger of not pulling out in time especially if there were hills in the area. We were usually about 1,000 ft (304 m) from the ground at the lowest point. We had to be that low to attain some degree of accuracy for our bombs. In a dive the altimeter was spinning around too fast to read how high we were, so it was purely a visual judgment that was required to avoid hitting the ground. All this was in addition to the chances of being hit by ground fire at any stage.

Pilot Wally Rutherford had acquired a pet chameleon called 'Gus' in North Africa and had taken it with him to Malta. He put this weird animal on the reflector gun sight of his Kitty for each trip and was very proud that the poor thing had survived the dive-bombing although the effect of 'G' on it had forced it into the bottom of the cockpit.

'Gus' the chamelion on Wally Rutherford's gun sight.
It survived several operational sorties

On Malta we were billeted in empty houses – a nice change from tents. Wally's 'Gus' lived with him in his room but tended to wander. Eventually it got lost. There followed a frantic search involving dozens of civilians and, despite a generous financial reward offered by Wally, the poor animal was never found.

In July 1943 after a few days operating from Malta we were able to land in Sicily at Pachino where the army had cleared the Jerries out of the south-eastern tip of the island for us. At Pachino landing ground we lived in new bivouacs, small tents that would take only one body, pitched among the vines and rife with mosquitoes. We still retained our EPIP mess tent. The German army had left only an hour or two previous to our landing and we were being shot at by remaining snipers. One particular nuisance had positioned himself high up in a water tower on the edge of the landing ground and was taking pot shots at us and our Kittys. We asked our own army, who were still around, to solve the problem for us. They promptly shot the sniper who fell dead into the water in the tower. This was a pity because we didn't fancy drinking the local water any more and had to resort to our own water bowsers once again.

Waiting for take-off, Pachino, Sicily, July 1943

We carried out armed recces from Pachino in support of our army. My first from there was to bomb and strafe a small harbour with some boats just south of Catania, causing a lot of damage. On that trip the flak was light and we all got back to base unscathed.

That night we were subjected to a bombing raid by Ju 88s. They didn't do much damage to us as their targets were mainly the army positions nearby but they did give us a sleepless night. On the 20th we had a cry for help from the 8th Army whose advance was held up by 88 mm guns and other enemy artillery emplacements. As we approached the area ready to bomb and strafe, we could see, even from a few thousand feet, the guns flashing from both sides as the battle raged. This gave us a clear indication of the Jerry positions, so down we went through a great deal of ack-ack from their light guns. It came up like a cloud of little white blobs and we had to continue through it and hope for the best. This time our bombs fell right on target (they didn't often) only a few hundred yards in front of our own 8th Army troops who were obviously having a bad time of it. We must have cheered them up considerably because on our return to base there was a signal from General Montgomery congratulating 112 Squadron with thanks for a job well done.

Next day our target was a goods train and station at Acireale. This time there was not much flak and after dive-bombing we went down to strafe. I was flying No 1 and the fifth Kitty to shoot up the train. The railway engine went up in a cloud of steam. Very satisfactory. Then we strafed the goods wagons. They didn't blow up so were not carrying explosives but we reckoned they would be of little use to the Jerries after we had gone.

Our next trip was to bomb the road and railway line to the west of Mount Etna. We called it 'going round the mountain', sometimes clockwise and sometimes anti-clockwise. The Jerries were not in favour of this strategy and answered with a lot of flak.

About this time Mussolini was deposed and his arrest ordered by the King of Italy.

One evening, at Pachino, we were amazed to see several USAAF four-engined Liberators circling around in the sky over us. Some of them were obviously in trouble with 'dead' props and gaping holes. They tried to land and eventually three got down on our strip, which was only just over 1,000 yards long (914 m). Others crashed on nearby landing strips.

They had returned from bombing oil fields at Ploesti in Rumania and had got completely lost. Some had even got back to North Africa, couldn't decide where they were and flew out to Sicily. Then they thought they were in Malta! Only the leading Liberator had a competent navigator and, of course, it got shot down leaving the others to fend for themselves. We didn't think this a very good system. The three crews were at the end of their tether and badly needed a rest. Our new CO, Squadron Leader

Our CO, Peter Illingworth

Preparing a Shark Squadron Kittyhawk for a sortie. Note the pierced steel planking (PSP) in the foreground

Peter Illingworth was quick to offer hospitality, so we dined and wined them in our mess tent and when they had finally passed out with the effect of a few drinks on top of their exhaustion, carried them off to camp beds for the night. Quite a party.

USAAF Liberator landing on the short grass runway at Pachino on return from the raid on the oil fields at Ploesti in Rumania

Next day all they wanted was a huge amount of petrol to see them on their way. Our petrol bowsers only held a few hundred gallons and they wanted thousands! Eventually we found them just enough to see them back to their North African bases. We held our breath as they took off with only inches to spare as they reached the end of the strip and pulled up over the vineyards.

The strips from which we operated in various locations in Sicily and Italy were constructed of PSP – Pierced Steel Planking. The army laid them out for us using tractors and small cranes. They were most effective and a great improvement on sandy landing grounds that we had previously used. Our tyres made a satisfactory zipping noise as we landed.

A crew that survived the Ploesti raid in happy mood at Pachino

The Spitfire Wing moved up to support us and gave us some top cover on occasions, although the air opposition from the Luftwaffe was now negligible. These Spits had an unusual experience one day in Sicily. They spotted a flight of four Italian Macchi 202 fighters and flew down on them out of the sun, only to find them waggling their wings and with flaps fully down. They were surrendering! The Spits led them back to the Spitfire base and sent the pilots off to prison camp.

I had a difficult personal experience. One day, strafing motor transport on a road 'around the mountain', I came across a motorcycle with dispatch rider driving at high speed. It was difficult strafing moving motor vehicles for the roads were narrow and twisting and, by the time I had got the Kitty into position to attack, the objective had nipped around another corner. I had a couple efforts at an attack. He must have got very frightened because he drove off the road, fell off his bike and ran across a field. I got into position to have another shot at him and as I came down to shoot, the Jerry stopped running and put up his hand in surrender!

I couldn't go through with it, so I let him go. But was this right? He lived to fight another day. Perhaps his dispatch was important to the enemy and if he'd been shot it wouldn't have reached its destination to the advantage of the Allied cause – we'll never know. This was a bit like the old question of whether to shoot a pilot falling in his parachute. One of the horrors of war. I don't think there is an answer – just do what seems best at the time.

My Kitty 'Z' was shared with other pilots, of course, and when I was not flying on the 26th my 'Z', which I had got so used to and which had seen me through all sorts of troubles, got shot down and the pilot killed.

The author seated in **GA-Z**

*A loose formation landing. Author in **GA-X**, almost a
three pointer but not quite*

On the 27th our target was MT, a factory and bridge at Castiglione.
I had to go in Kitty 'X'. We dive-bombed and this time felt everything was
going just right with the dive and my release of the bomb. Sure enough my
bomb and others landed on the bridge, which was completely demolished.
It was not easy to demolish a whole bridge with a few bombs from a few
thousand feet, so this was a better than usual result – very satisfactory.

On the 31st Pilot Officer Wild and myself went strafing near
Randazzo and came across Jerry MT and a tank on the road. Two lorries
burst into flames but the tank, although hit by both Reg and myself, just
would not burn. It must have been unpleasant inside with .5 inch bullets
banging on the outside! Flak started coming up, so we cleared off.

Our Army now had control over all south-east Sicily and was
advancing on the town of Catania, half way up the east coast. A strip of
lava and volcanic ash was prepared for us in a marshy area at Agnone, just

a few miles south of Catania. On 2 August we gave close army support with a dive-bombing on Jerry within sight of our troops. We fired our guns on the way down as well as dropping our bombs, so the Jerries were at the end of a frightening attack. To me it was exhilarating firing and bombing at the same time. I only had to look out for empty shells from the Kitty in front. Only small arms fire came at us this time and we all survived to land at our new strip: Agnone.

CHAPTER TWELVE

GROUP CAPTAIN 'JACKIE' DARWEN DFC

Agnone was only a few miles south of Catania. In August 1943 we camped there around the strip in a mosquito swamp and found it quite unbearable. On top of a hill overlooking the strip was a small abandoned Italian army camp consisting of two large huts, one with a glass room on top and some abandoned field guns with ammunition. This, we felt, would be better than in the swamp. The only problem was that there were bodies of several dead soldiers to be cleared away. Our MO and Padre organized the clearing up and when all was smelling sweet and clean we moved our living tents up the hill. I thought I would 'get away from it all' at nights by sleeping in the glass room on top of the hut we used as the pilots' and officers' lounge/bar. The other hut was our dining room. The lounge/bar sounds very civilized, however drinks were very limited and consisted mostly of Chianti and a great variety of sickly liquors purloined from an abandoned hotel.

The officer commanding our 239 Wing of Kittyhawk squadrons was Group Captain 'Jackie' Darwen DFC and, like our squadron CO, was a regular RAF officer. There was therefore a common interest between them, and the Group Captain spent many evenings in our mess together with Peter and any RAF characters who happened to be visiting the Wing such as Group Captain 'Cockie' Dundas, Wing Commander Billy Drake (both veterans of the Battle of Britain) and others. Jackie Darwen therefore adopted our 112 Shark Squadron as his own and flew with us quite frequently leading us into battle.

*The dining room at the Italian artillery camp with author's
temporary bedroom on top. Agonoe, August 1943*

The lounge with two artillery pieces overlooking Catania harbour

The operations tent, Agnone, Sicily. The 'Gaggle Board' is on the left

Jackie had been dancing with his wife in London's Café de Paris when a German bomb fell killing many. His wife died in his arms. It was not surprising then that he hated the Germans almost to a disproportionate amount. When in action he had total disregard for his own safety, pressing home his attacks in a fever to kill as many Jerries as possible. His avowed greatest wish was to find a queue of them at their cookhouse door and kill them all with a burst of gunfire. He claimed that he had got one sitting on a toilet bucket. It was rather frightening to hear him talk like this. He joined in our mess 'parties', often in his Hunting Pink, which he regarded as an essential part of his kit in memory of peacetime pleasures.

In action, when he had Jerry in his sights, he found it difficult to take his finger off the firing trigger with the result that, on his return, the armourers had to cope with melted gun barrels. We had learned to keep to three-second bursts to let the barrels cool.

Jackie had a jeep to drive around in, which he did at high speed, bouncing over the rough track down the hill between our mess and the airstrip. One day I saw him bounce his jeep up onto a rock so that no wheel

The Adjutant in his 'office'

was touching the ground – he revved up but nothing happened. He had to get four of us to lift the vehicle off the rock so he could get going again. He was a most refreshing character to have known but a little frightening to fly with.

Operations against the Jerries at this time were almost always through heavy flak, both from their 88 mm guns, from 40 mm Breda and even small arms fire from 20 mm down to hand guns. At this time we sometimes flew in smaller formations, usually in fours without bombs. We had specific areas to attack but could use our judgment in finding targets to strafe when we got there. We called these trips 'Rhubarbs' as they seemed to have the same effect on our bowels! We flew as pairs with the leader covered by his No 2 and another No 1 with his cover weaving behind him. In this way we attacked with little risk of being surprised from the rear. Although at this time there was little opposition from the Luftwaffe.

I was flying on one of these Rhubarbs on 3 August, each of us with a No 2 to guard our tails. We strafed roads west of Mount Etna and right up the north coast of the island. I got four 'flamers' (vehicles that were seen to burn) on the way and several damaged which would not burst into flames. We found some Jerry gun positions on the coast and set about destroying them. Naturally they threw all they could at us and I received a direct hit damaging my aileron controls. I had nearly run out of ammunition anyway so headed for home. Flight Sergeant 'Artie' Shaw shadowed me back to Agnone to make sure I got back all right. I have a note in my logbook which says "Thanks Artie". On inspection back at base I realized I had been hit by two 40 mm shells. Reg Wilde did not return on this trip but later turned up having force-landed on an American Air Force strip in the north of the island with his damaged Kitty.

While we lost a number of pilots and their Kittys in this campaign, there were some remarkable escapes. The Kittyhawk took a lot of punishment. Two such escapes were so remarkable that many of us took photographs of the damaged aircraft. Reg Drown brought back one Kitty when enemy flak had blown great holes in his wing, damaging, but not exploding, 40 lb (18 kg) anti-personnel bombs hanging under.

Reg Drown's narrow escape with no less than two shells having passed through his port wing, narrowly missing the underslung 40lb (18kg) anti-personnel bombs

*The view from below the wing. The fin of one of the
40lb anti-personnel bombs can be seen to the left*

Flight Lieutenant Bluett had seventy-five percent of his fin and rudder shot away and still got back – just! The illustration shows this compared with a full fin and rudder.

The Germans must have realized they would have to pull out of Sicily and in a desperate effort to protect their retreating army had amassed a great barrage of anti-aircraft guns, even bringing in extra fire power from Italy.

As close as it gets. Flak damage to Reg Drown's Kittyhawk, a round passing through the port wing and mangling but not detonating one of the 40lb bombs on the underwing racks

*Flying Officer Matthias was flying **GA-D** 'Don' when a round passed through his fin*

Left is shown a replacement fin and rudder. Right is the remaining piece of rudder with which Flight Lieutenant Bluett had to fly back

Shark Squadron flight coming in to land on completion of an operation

They also made a last effort to wipe out the Desert Air Force so that they could complete the evacuation of Sicily without great losses. On the evening of the 11th, just after dark, we witnessed from the hilltop an RAF night-fighter, a Beaufighter we learned later, shooting down a German aircraft which came down in flames and burnt itself out on the beach nearby. Then a full raid by Ju 88s was upon us. First, flares dropped all around to light up our Kittys parked for the night. Our RAF Regiment gunners opened up in reply. Those who had tin hats put them on and we all took cover to watch the show, watching helplessly as the raid progressed. Jerry dropped green flares to light up their target and then the bombs rained down. It was quite a change to be on the receiving end of an air raid and was very spectacular. I was thinking how lucky we were to be up on the hill, just outside the target area, when Jackie Darwen ordered everyone down to the airstrip to put out fires. Many Kittys were punctured by shrapnel and one of our Corporal ground staff was killed by one of the bombs which were still coming down as he attempted to put out the fires. Another airman was severely injured. The fires were mainly caused by incendiaries setting fire to dry undergrowth and, surprisingly, most Kittys were spared serious damage. In half an hour it was all over. By midday on the 12th we were back to full strength.

The Spitfire Wing also got a pasting that night and several Spits were written off.

I decided my little glass eyrie on top of the mess hut was not a safe place to sleep if we were to have this sort of attention from Jerry, so brought my kit down smartly and settled for a tent again.

Next day we took off on a Rhubarb of four with Jackie Darwen leading and myself flying at his side. No doubt Jackie was looking for revenge. We strafed the coast road under very heavy fire from guns on the cliffs. Jackie led us out to sea and back, getting down almost to nought feet over the water and came in with a roar at the guns on the cliff, firing all the way. I saw a flash on Jackie's Kitty engine and thought for a moment he was finished. On the way back his aircraft looked peculiar but I couldn't quite make out what was wrong. On landing and inspection, his propeller boss, the big red bit at the front, had been completely shot off!

CHAPTER THIRTEEN

NIGHT FLYING AND THE 'PISSIES'

Many operations at this time were around the Mount Etna area, often in Rhubarbs of four, just strafing any MT or other targets we could find. One such was to the Randazzo area led by Flying Officer 'Goose' Guess RCAF where we left many trucks burning. As we came around the side of the volcano we got shot at by Jerry light guns. Ray Guess did not get back. He was the pilot who had shot down Heinz Ludemann, the Me 109 pilot, in North Africa. Later we learned that Ray was a POW. I never did find out why he was called 'Goose'.

Occasionally we did a trip to the toe of Italy mostly looking for shipping. We found a very large barge in the Gulf of Gioia that looked as though it could be used for Jerry troops and dropped our 500lb bombs. All twelve of them missed so we went down to strafe. We used up a lot of ammunition but eventually it caught fire and beached. I caught some flak from the mainland and heard a great thump behind me. I flew back OK and found a big hole through the fuselage of 'W', the Kitty I was flying that trip. It had missed the battery and the flying controls by fractions of an inch. I got someone to take a photograph of the hole with myself, looking proudly on. The owner of Kitty 'W' said he wouldn't lend me his precious Kitty again but he was overruled and I flew it next day – a full squadron with 500 lb (227 kg) bombs and led by Jackie Darwen with Flight Lieutenant Bluett leading the top six. I was in Bluett's six and after sinking a large ferry boat and strafing a tug, we were led in at nought feet over the sea to attack enemy guns firing at us from the cliff tops again.

Bluett led our six back at 200ft (61 m) over the front line, presenting a gratuitous target, and we got shot at again. I didn't think this was a good tactic.

*The author in the background surveys the starboard side of the damage inflicted on **GA-W** 'William'. The 'owner' was not amused but I flew it again the next day*

Jackie Darwen didn't like coming back with any ammo left, so we had spent a nail-biting long time over the target. This time we were so late back that when we got over the airstrip at Agnone it was quite dark. Of course we had no night flying equipment in the Kittys or on the ground. However the ground staff arranged all possible trucks to line up around the strip with headlights on to give us a chance. There were several hairy landings including mine. What with one thing and another I was faintly surprised that we all got back, albeit with a few holes here and there. So night-flying training back at EFTS, SFTS and OTU had not been in vain.

On the 13th we flew another operation aimed at shipping off the mainland in the Gulf of Gioia. We dived-bombed an E-boat and small barge, both targets getting direct hits. On the return journey, we attacked a Blohm & Voss 138 seaplane on the water and a Ju 52 trying to take off from a beach. Both were destroyed.

We came back via the Straits of Messina which were now becoming very unhealthy indeed. It was said that it had the biggest concentration of ack-ack in all Europe for the two weeks of the German withdrawal from Sicily. Thirty-five heavy batteries as well as numerous light batteries were positioned there. This trip was very frustrating because we had no bombs and little ammo left to fire, so we couldn't have a go at some barges and a large ship seen just leaving Messina harbour.

Martin Barnes OC 112 Squadron Field Battery

While still at Agnone we heaved two of the artillery pieces out of their dugouts and set them up outside the mess hut pointing out over the bay of Catania. Martin Barnes had been in the artillery in the army before re-mustering as a pilot, so was appointed OC 112 Squadron Field Battery. There was plenty of ammunition lying around so some practice at loading and unloading was carried out, everyone having a go like children with a new toy. At last one evening the desire to fire these guns got the better of us but we didn't like to ask permission in case it was refused, which seemed highly likely, so we hit on a cunning plan. That evening Jackie Darwen and cronies, as well as ourselves, were having a 'party' in the mess. The OC Field Battery handed Jackie a piece of string and suggested he pull it. He did just that and there was a terrific bang as the two 25-pounders went off, sending shells screaming out into the bay. At first Jackie was indignant that the guns had been fired without his authority, but when he realized that it was he who had fired them, he thought it great fun and more shots were fired. Eventually a signal came through to us from the Royal Navy anchored in Catania Harbour saying they would reply with 12 inch shells if we continued to make them nervous!

As the Jerry ack-ack got fiercer we had a problem with a colleague of ours. He kept returning from sorties before reaching the scene of action. We all had an occasional faulty engine or radio but this pilot, "Malcolm Barnaby" I'll call him, had so many that it became obvious he had 'gone LMF' as we put it. One day it was a radio fault that cured itself on getting back to base. Another day it was an engine that "sounded rough" but no fault could be found by the fitter, and so on week after week.

The ground staff had a nickname for most pilots. I never did find out what mine was – perhaps it is just as well! Anyway, this pilot was naturally known as 'Boomerang Barnaby'. Some pilots became quite upset at his behaviour, reckoning he was "letting the side down" and "if we all did that the war would be lost" and so on. Some, in disgust, would hardly speak to him at all. Personally, I was in two minds about it. For one thing, 'Barnaby' was a married man with wife and baby girl. This set him apart from most of us who were single young men about 20–22 years old. He talked about his family incessantly and that was understandable. I had the feeling, because of this family back home, he found it more difficult to face up to the prospect of being killed than we did. So I had a little sympathy for him. At least he had joined up to have a go. I had to keep my thoughts to myself as colleagues got very bitter about it – some are, even to this day.

I have often wondered whether we were brave or if we were more afraid of being thought a coward than we were of dying? If so then perhaps 'Barnaby' was more afraid of leaving his family than he was of being thought a coward. Eventually the CO had him posted away and that was the end of the problem as far as we were concerned.

While operating from Agnone there was a lull in the fighting and as there were no more operations for us that day, five of us pilots decided to see what the town of Catania had to offer. We piled into a 13cwt truck and set off up the main road. There had been some bloody fighting along this route only the previous days and the stench of battle hung heavily. Several funeral pyres were burning at the side of the road and a Padre was reading a prayer at one of them. The sickening smell of burning bodies took a long time to get out of one's nostrils and out of memory, never. We didn't have to cope with this sort of problem often in the RAF.

The road fromAgnone to Catania which had been the scene of heavy fighting only hours before this photograph was taken. A wrecked British glider lies beside the road

We were glad to reach Catania although it was quite badly damaged having fallen to the 8th Army only the previous day or so. All was quiet, the streets almost deserted. We wandered around beginning to think there was not much to see when one pilot shouted: "Come and look at this!" He was peering through a crack in some warehouse doors and we all crowded around for a look. There were aeroplanes in there – several of them!

This was exciting stuff so it didn't take many minutes to break in and take stock of our find.

There were wings, fuselages and engines, enough to make up six or seven light aircraft. We found paperwork and realized that they were Caproni 100s of the Catania Flying Club. They were very much like Tiger Moths with Gipsy Moth engines, built under licence, no doubt.

It was very clear that there was fun to be had from these spoils of war if only we could transport them back to Agnone.

That night in the pilots' mess in the old Italian army hut, we told the CO and Jackie Darwen of our find in Catania. After getting all the details, it didn't take Jackie many moments to make his decision. He picked up the field telephone: "Bunch call, all squadrons. I want a convoy of 3-ton trucks into Catania at first light. Bring back all the Caproni parts".

So it came about that 112 'Shark' Squadron had two flying condition Caproni 100s on its strength. The balance of the find was divided, one Caproni each around the squadrons on the Wing. Two for the 'Shark' squadron because we had found them. The fitters and riggers assembled them and on 24 August I got my first solo trip in a Caproni 100 to enter in my log book.

A Caproni 100 arriving at the landing ground which had been cleared by Shark Squadron on the slopes of Mount Etna

Caproni 100 of the Catania Flying Club airborne with 'Taffy' the Adjutant in the front cockpit, August 1943. Note the unique squadron coding

Both pilots and ground staff enjoyed 'playing' with the Capronis

There was one awesome difference from a Tiger Moth or any other aircraft we had flown – the throttle worked the other way round. We had to pull it back to increase power! This, of course, led to some hairy flying, especially landings. It was quite difficult to remember to push the throttle forward to cut the engine! The wheels were like pram wheels and angled inwards in flight. They assumed normal attitude on landing.

The ground staff were delighted. In return for assembling the Capronis and painting GA–1 and GA–2 on the fuselages, we were able to give them passenger trips in between continuing ops. Even Taffy, the Adjutant, enjoyed a gentle flight in the sunshine. Kittyhawks were, of course, single seaters so we had been unable to take passengers previously. My fitter Nick was particularly grateful. It was the least I could do after the conscientious way he looked after my Kittyhawk. I'd never had any serious engine problems. During the next two weeks we had a lot of fun with these lovely light aircraft, between our continuing operations against the enemy. We called them the 'Pissies' as they were good for 'pissing about in' and we even went shopping in them to pick up a few delicacies for the mess.

*Our hotel 'rest centre' on the slopes of Mount
Etna, scene of many memorable 'bashes'*

We found a deserted hotel on the side of Mount Etna and, most importantly, discovered some hooch in the cellar. It was rather inaccessible until the CO gave permission to clear a landing area adjacent so we could transport our delighted fellow pilots to the hotel in the Capronis. There were some happy parties there.

*Reg Drown managed to even the score for his badly damaged
Kittyhawk with an Me 109 G*

Our previous CO, Squadron Leader George Norton, had been killed in this area flying from Malta and we used the Capronis in an attempt to find his crashed Kittyhawk. One of our pilots was eventually successful. George's crash site and grave were located and details entered in the records for the benefit of his next of kin.

Of course our fun with the Capronis couldn't last. When we advanced to the Italian mainland to continue the war with the Germans, we had to leave those lovely Caproni 100s behind us.

CHAPTER FOURTEEN

THE STRAITS OF MESSINA – SKIP BOMBING

The very name gave us pilots a feeling of dread and yet it was our job to prevent, as much as possible, the enemy from escaping from Messina across the straits to San Giovanni on the mainland through a cloud of ack-ack right up to 8,000 ft (2438 m). It came up at us from both shores. The Jerries were using quite modern Siebel ferries to get their army across and if we got near enough there would be a shower of small arms fire from the troops aboard.

Some days the squadron flew thirty-six sorties; sometimes dive bombing, sometimes just strafing. Dive-bombing meant penetrating the heavier 88 mm fire, then the 40 mm and, before pulling out, the 20 mm and small arms fire with little chance of sinking a ferry. We sank a few ferries and barges through the intense fire, although no one pilot could claim a particular success. They were team efforts. These operations were difficult and I began to be a bit depressed about the possibility of surviving or not. I think others felt the same. The atmosphere in the pilots' mess was a little subdued for these few days.

It was because of these problems that Jackie Darwen came up with an innovative idea for sinking shipping in the straits. He called it 'skip bombing' and he was set on trying it out. The idea was to approach the shipping broadside on from sea level, releasing our 500 lb (226 kg) bombs so they would 'skip' across the water into the side of the enemy ship. The whole idea seemed wild and fraught with great danger to me.

Jackie talked it over with us in the mess one evening and we had no alternative but to say we would have a go. Next day Jackie led a flight of six of us – skip bombing. We six flew steadily out to sea parallel with the east coast and as low over the sea as we could get, heading for the dreaded straits. Our No 2s complained that they couldn't get below their No 1s' slipstream we were so low. I was so tensed up with fright that I found myself gripping the joystick with white knuckles, all sorts of dreadful possibilities going through my mind. Suddenly, I saw a school of porpoise in the water ahead of us. I thought nothing of it – my thoughts were elsewhere – when on the R/T the unmistakable voice of Jackie came over: "Oh, what lovely porpoise. Did you see those?" Suddenly, I had a terrific feeling of anti-climax. Here was I thinking only of a faint possibility of surviving the trip at all, and here was the Group Captain admiring the bloody porpoise. I laughed hysterically – the only time I can remember laughing out loud during an op.

We did achieve surprise. Right in front of us were two barges full of troops, broadside on. Jackie released his bomb first. It broke into fragments on its first impact with the water, fortunately without exploding. The rest of our bombs just disappeared into the water.

Small arms fire became intense but the main ack-ack guns were not firing, so Jackie pulled up and around to have a strafing run at the barges. We followed suit and a few moments battle with the troops aboard followed. I felt very sorry to see one of our Kittys catch fire. The Aussie pilot pulled up and eventually baled out. Quickly we pulled away, leaving one barge on fire, and headed for base. Later, from other bombers, we learned that the barge was sinking, so not a completely unsuccessful trip.

The next day Jackie led another skip bombing trip. This time without me – glad to say. This time they attempted to pull up at the last minute and drop bombs directly on to the target ship. It was amazing that no Kitty blew itself up. Fortunately Jackie decided it didn't really work and abandoned the idea.

Jackie was the bane of the ground crews as he never returned without some damage. He had GA–JD painted on his shark Kitty. Once he came back with his propeller tips bent, having struck the top of a German vehicle. He was not the only one who flew low on strafing runs. Ken Middlemist came back with telegraph wires wrapped around his engine cowling – he had hit a telegraph pole while strafing.

On the 18th, in Kitty 'X', I went on an armed recce around the toe of Italy and found a loaded train at Melito. We dive bombed with 500-pounders and left several trucks ablaze. The railway engine refused to blow up. I got some holes in my wings but there were no losses that time.

On the 27th we set off to escort Mitchell bombers to a target on the mainland. My engine started to vibrate inexplicably so turned back just before the target area and returned to base. This was the first time I had ever returned early from an op and felt badly about it. My fitter Nick could find little wrong with the engine – it only needed tuning up a bit. I began to wonder if I was getting twitchy.

On 7 September Italy surrendered and on the 12th we flew to the mainland to support the invasion of Italy itself. I had flown fifty-one operations with the Shark Squadron so far.

CHAPTER FIFTEEN

CAPTURING AN AIRPORT

Whether it was a rumour or just propaganda to boost our morale, I don't know, but we began to believe that when we got to the mainland of Italy we would be accommodated in top class hotels with hot and cold running maids, etc. In the event, we had to camp in the open air under mosquito nets hung from the branches of trees. The place was called Grottaglie and was on the main road between Taranto and Brindisi.

Our 'luxury' hotel on the mainland turned out to be a group of mosquito nets with camp beds in an olive grove between Taranto and Brindisi

The whole operation was supported by a squadron of DC-3s (Dakotas) of the USAAC. They flew the advanced party, with some light equipment and three or four of us pilots who were not flying our Kittys, across to Grottaglie escorted by 260 Squadron Kittys. The DC-3s continued to support us with food, water, ammo, bombs, glycol and so on for a week until the full equipment arrived by sea. Until then the ground staff had to pump petrol by hand from 40 gallon (180 ltr) drums into our aircraft. Our trucks and petrol bowsers did not arrive for a week and in the meantime bombs and ammo had to be manhandled to the aircraft. I believe it was a bit of history as we were the first operational squadron to be supported entirely by air.

We were the first Kittyhawk squadron to arrive on the mainland and for a while the DC-3s and 112 Squadron had the landing ground to ourselves. Just as well because it was nearly as dusty as the desert had been. We had to take off in formation leaving the dust to settle for twenty minutes or so before anyone else could use it.

The day after arriving, the 17th, we were operational again. Six of us took off in formation each carrying two 250 lb (113 kg) bombs slung under the fuselage as our work was to destroy any enemy MT we could find on or near the roads. This time we found twenty-plus vehicles and two tanks on a road to the north west of Potenza. The roads in this area were very twisty and moving targets difficult to hit. This time, however, the German troops, except the tank crews, ran from their vehicles leaving them to us. We dive bombed successfully, the bombs falling in among the MT. There was no ack-ack coming up at us so we went down for several strafing runs. Only light small-arms fire from the troops was experienced. One target looked like a staff car, so I made a special run at that and left it and several others burning. Other 'Shark' pilots, of course, had similar successes.

To be on the receiving end of our six .5 inch (12.7mm) guns, especially with explosive bullets, must have been terrible and devastating. We switched our guns to 'live' well before reaching our target area. The gun trigger itself was on the joystick. When this was pulled it felt as if the 'brakes' had been applied, the recoil was so great. I mention this because, says my diary, on this day I saw Jerries being thrown across the road by our bullets. I was coming down to strafe alongside another Kitty which was firing at some Jerries who were leaning over the parapet of a small bridge aiming rifles at us. I saw my colleague's fire hit the Jerries knocking them across the road and over the parapet at the far side.

We carried out several of these bombing and strafing trips to support our 7th Armoured Division on their bridgehead at Salerno not so far away to the west. Sometimes we had a lot of flak to contend with; in other areas we found targets without this cover. We had to be very careful strafing near the Salerno bridgehead because the position on the ground was very fluid. I remember strafing a road to find several horse-drawn trailers of supplies for the Jerries in my sights. I could see the horses rearing up in fright. I hadn't the stomach to fire at them so I cleared off to strafe elsewhere. Maybe those supplies were vital to Jerry and I should have done my duty.

We lost Ken Middlemist and Staveley, both shot down and killed while strafing, over those few days from Grottaglie. Also on the 19th 'Western Desert' Brown was hit at about 1,500ft (457 m) and he spun into the ground in flames. He was one of the most experienced pilots in the Shark Squadron at that time and was almost 'tour expired'. He was the one who had shot down Heinz Ludemann back in the desert. Experience did not help avoid the ack-ack fire once we were attacking.

On the 18th I flew in Jackie Darwen's 'JD' Kitty. He told me not to get shot down that trip, because he wanted it back! I shared several MT 'flamers' with Johnnie Burcham. On the 19th our flight of six Kittys was led by Spitfires to a Jerry ammo and petrol dump at Spinazzola surrounded by ack-ack. We dived-bombed with 250-pounders and then strafed. Several big fires resulted then there was a huge explosion – quite spectacular. Personally, I concentrated on their ack-ack gun emplacements around the dump. I certainly destroyed one emplacement with its gun and crew. At the end of this action we landed back at our new base – Brindisi.

This aerodrome, complete with hangars, had been a large base for the *Regia Aeronautica* (Italian airforce) and there were many aircraft still there – some in working order. Also there were two or three Italian pilots hanging around.

Another Italian pilot flew in with a Macchi 202 fighter. He had escaped from the Jerries up north and wanted to join us. We invited him into the mess for an occasional 'party' and he became our interpreter. We were not prepared to let him fly with us. Also on the aerodrome were a Fieseler *Storch*, two or three Savoia–Marchetti 82s and others. We were not sure at that time whether they were booby-trapped so we couldn't fly them till they had been checked by the army. By that time we had moved on.

We carried out several armed recces from Brindisi. One evening, after the day's operations, we went into the town to see what it had to offer and ended up in an hotel on the sea-front overlooking the harbour. Several Allied ships had arrived there to supply the 1st Airborne Division. This hotel was about the only one with a bar, doing a roaring trade with Army lads, nurses and ourselves. A joint-services party developed. One of our pilots was standing on a table singing the numerous verses of Sweet Angeline, all joining in the choruses, when we realized that an air-raid was developing outside. Soon it became obvious the Jerries were aiming to bomb shipping in the harbour, and with some accuracy.

There was a great curve of glass window around this hotel bar/lounge looking out over the harbour and we felt very vulnerable to flying glass so I lay down under a heavy table. This proved to be a good move because there was a tremendous explosion as one of the ammo ships blew up and the whole of the glass front of the hotel blew in with glass splinters everywhere. Fortunately everyone had got right down on the floor so there were not many serious casualties. The nurses, who a few minutes before had been joining in the singing, were busy patching up our wounds from the flying glass and splinters of window frame. Fortunately, I only got a few scratches myself. As soon as the raid was over, we 112 Squadron pilots piled into our truck and headed back to the aerodrome.

The 1st Airborne Division was rapidly pushing the Jerries back so, on the 22nd, Taffy the Adjutant, with a small party of ground staff, set off for Bari which was to be our next base. He carried an R/T set and could communicate with us while we were flying.

On this day we had instructions to land at Bari Airport on our return from an armed recce. I was flying No 2 to Bluett in a flight of six. Taffy called us up to say that, on approaching Bari Airport, they had come across soldiers of the 1st Airborne Division who were still trying to clear the enemy from around the perimeter and that it would be unwise to land. So we circled around for a few minutes until we had little petrol left and then decided to land and risk it. Bluett, as leader, should have landed first, of course, but he was intent on looking for German positions to strafe on the outskirts of the airport, instructing me to land with the other four and await his arrival. I did this and had the privilege of being the first Allied aircraft to 'liberate' the airport. I taxied in towards the hangars with the others following. I warily climbed out clutching my revolver, wondering what reception committee might be waiting. A group of *Regia Aeronautica* officers approached and I was very relieved to see they had their hands out in friendly welcome. Bluett joined us and so we accepted the surrender of Bari Airport. We didn't get shot at after all but we could hear a battle proceeding much too near for our liking. However, in an hour or so the Jerries had been completely cleared from the area.

CHAPTER SIXTEEN

CAB-RANK

Flying from Bari on 24 September we set out at the request of the Army to bomb the town of Melfi. Apparently some Jerry troops were hiding there. This was the first time that I had bombed a town without a more specific target. We believed all the citizens had cleared out. All bombs fell in the town, and rightly, it was a large target! This trip was unusual in that we encountered no ack-ack, no enemy aircraft – just a simple flight without incident, fifty-five minutes. The army was pleased anyway.

On the 26th we were back on MT bombing and strafing near Avellino; back to usual light ack-ack and small arms fire from unhappy Jerries. We left several vehicles burning and many more damaged.

We didn't stay long at Bari. We only did four ops from there. All were armed recces on Jerry transport. We noted movements, direction and concentration of enemy vehicles and our IO passed on the information to the army who found it useful.

I had my eye on a camera shop in Brindisi and, not being needed for ops one day at the end of September, asked permission to pop back in a Kitty to see if it was now opened up. I pointed out to the CO that my Kitty 'Z' needed an air test and he agreed. In Brindisi the shop was still shut but next door told me where to locate the owner and got him to open up for me. He'd got a German Leica 35 mm camera there and when he saw that I really wanted it, asked a huge price. I had to threaten to requisition it for the use of the RAF till after the war to persuade him to talk more reasonably. Eventually thought I got a fair deal, so took it back to the aerodrome, climbed into my Kitty and returned to the Squadron to have my purchase much admired by colleagues. From that time on, many of the illustrations in this book were taken by me with this Leica.

In early October we advanced to Foggia. This city had fallen to the 1st Airborne Division only a few days earlier. There was a large grass aerodrome with one runway, littered with wrecked Jerry aircraft. Also there were several satellite landing grounds – a very useful capture. On 4 October we tried to carry out an armed recce from the now cleared Foggia Main but the weather was bad and we had to turn back without dropping our bombs.

Author (left) with Ray Hearn in the 3-ton 'Ops. Room'

In North Africa, Warrant Officer Smith, our engineer, had invented and designed a special bomb rack for the Kitty to carry two 250lb (113 kg) bombs under the fuselage and at about this time he received the MBE for his work (see page 61). These 250-pounders were useful for anti-person-nel and anti-MT work. When we were to attack these targets our armour-ers would fit the bomb nose-caps with 12 inch or 18 inch (30 or 45 cm) rods to lift the explosion level and cause maximum damage.

In North Africa the weather was so good we didn't need our artificial horizons on the instrument panel. When it was decided to uplift the bomb-load to two 500-pounders under the wings the authorities decided to remove the artificial horizon and other equipment to compensate for the additional bomb-load. Among other measures, they fitted a very small electric battery instead of the large capacity one in the fuselage. The heavy steel wheels were replaced by aluminium ones.

Now we carried a 500 lb (226 kg) bomb under the fuselage and two more 500-pounders under the wings. This total of 1,500 lbs (680 kg) caused us to take off with some flap and to stand on the brakes until the revs had mounted up before moving forward.

Now in Italy, with winter drawing near, the weather was different and suddenly we needed that artificial horizon again! Also we had continuous trouble from a battery behind the seat, too small to cope with all the 'electrics'. So the instruments were put back in and the full sized battery reinstated. The aluminium wheels occasionally cracked under the additional weight of bombs, so we went back to steel wheels. Then, would you believe, we were persuaded to try a 1,000 lb (453 kg) bomb under the fuselage. So now we carried, on special occasions, 2,000 lbs (907 kg) of bombs. This was nearly as much as the B-25 Mitchells that we escorted!

We explored the city of Foggia with the idea of finding suitable accommodation for the pilots and officers. It was a deserted city. Rumour had it that Churchill had threatened to destroy this city in revenge for the bombing of Coventry, if the Italians would not capitulate. Whether this was true or not, certainly the Italians had capitulated a few weeks earlier and the city had not been bombed. However the entire population had fled to the hills. The city had been looted, presumably by the Jerries. There were many apartment blocks. Each one had been broken into and individual flats plundered. Often entry had been made by smashing through the wall, rather than opening or breaking down the door. The weird thing was that many flats had been abandoned in the middle of a meal, half eaten food left on plates.

Eventually we found a flat that was in good condition with plenty of furniture and a radiogram. We drove backwards and forwards from the flat to the aerodrome by truck while the NCOs and men were encamped in tents on the airfield.

In the flat at Foggia. The height of luxury!
Eddie Ross (left) with Johnnie Burcham

On 5 October the weather had improved so we set off to assist the 8th Army. They were held down by Jerries in a wooded valley near Termoli. The German Panzer Division was here, about to launch a counter attack. Again we carried 250 pounders (113 kg) and this time our aim was good, all bombs falling into the target area. Much 40 mm and 20 mm ack-ack was encountered as we dived down below 4,000 ft (1219 m). We always had fierce opposition from Jerry tanks. This time I sustained only small shrapnel holes. I could hear the clang-clang of them hitting my metal Kitty 'Z' as I pulled out of my dive. We all got back safely after only about fifty minutes in the air, to find a signal from the 8th Army saying that we had done well and that, as a result of our bombing, thirty German paratroops had surrendered!

Unfortunately we heard that on another trip, flying over the Foggia area, Jackie Darwen had been shot down by 88 mm fire. He was flying at about 8,000 ft (2438 m) and had a direct hit with no chance of survival. There was a memorial service for him on the 10th, but I didn't go. Best just to look to the future.

Next day we flew further to the Capua area where we found twenty-plus MT on the road. There was terrific 88 mm ack-ack. We had these black bursts among us as we got in position to dive. The Kitty P-40 had a large radiator filled with glycol coolant under the engine, which made us vulnerable to an unlucky shrapnel hit. If the glycol poured out the engine would soon overheat and seize up and a forced landing or baling out followed. Quite a few pilots had this experience and, because of the mountainous terrain, usually bailed out.

Our parachute packer was Flight Sergeant Jock Crawford, a dour Scot, and to our knowledge he never had a failure. In recognition of this record he was twice 'Mentioned in Dispatches'. On this trip, one of our new pilots had to bale out, hopefully to survive to become a POW or even escape.

Sergeant 'Jock' Crawford our parachute packer at work.
He was twice mentioned in dispatches

We soon got to learn the various types of ack-ack thrown up at us. 88 mm could reach us at over 8,000 ft (2438 m) and came in big black puffs with a red centre to be seen if close enough. Lower down, Breda guns would open up with tracers and smaller white puffs. Often we could see a whole layer of these white puffs below us in the dive and we just had to continue down through it to release our bombs and pull up, again through a layer of gunfire. However, occasionally we did a whole trip including dive-bombing and strafing without any opposition at all.

Over the next few days we carried out several ops to support the army, often attacking enemy gun positions or tanks and MT on the roads. On the 22nd we did a longer distance armed recce with 40 lb (18 kg) bombs under the wings and a long-range belly tank. I saw some trucks hiding under camouflage just off the road and asked permission of the leader to attack. He said "OK" so myself and No 2 went down to strafe. It was a staff car and a few trucks and we strafed with only small arms fire to contend with. We left them burning. Then we had a job to catch up with the squadron formation again but eventually succeeded. We were in the air nearly two hours.

On the 25th, with long-range tanks again, we went to Yugoslavia to bomb and strafe German invasion barges that were attacking the island of Korcula held by the Patriots. The barges looked empty to me and there was no opposition. It seemed a long way over the Adriatic and I never did feel comfortable over the sea. I suppose I didn't like the idea of getting wet. Anyway my engine always sounded rough as we lost sight of land!

On the 26th we flew our Kittys to a new landing ground at a satellite landing ground called Melini, five miles away. On the west coast our 7th Armoured Division had entered Naples.

I had now completed over seventy operational sorties during the last seven months with 112 Squadron and was becoming quite experienced. So far I had only led four Kittys on a Rhubarb. I felt I could cope with leading the whole squadron of twelve Kittys into battle, but "not yet" said the CO.

Near the Melini landing ground was an unoccupied farmhouse – just right for our living quarters. The weather was getting colder and damper so we gathered in much timber to make a roaring fire under the old farmhouse chimney. We bought some chestnuts to roast and generally made ourselves as comfortable as possible. There was not much sleeping accommodation in the farmhouse for all the officers and pilots, so some of us slept in tents or in outhouses. Eddy Ross made a bath from a ground-sheet suspended in a manger in one of the outhouses.

The farm buildings at Melini, December 1943

Away in a manger - Eddie Ross in his 'patent' bath

For us to dive-bomb and strafe it was essential to have a reasonably high cloud base and through this December in Southern Italy these conditions were rarely met, so I have little flying activity to talk about until January when I flew another seventeen ops in the month. However, there were interesting developments. In particular, it was about this time that we began to develop the 'Cab-Rank' system of close army support. The idea was that soldiers on the ground could contact Kittyhawks flying above and direct them to bomb and strafe exactly where needed.

In practice it was started by Group Captain David Hayson whose code name was 'Rover'. He was installed in a forward ground Observation Post, usually overlooking the enemy positions. He worked closely with the Army Commander and between them would instruct the Kittyhawks waiting overhead to bomb and/or strafe a particular point identified by similar gridded map references both in the hands of Rover David and each pilot above.

The Kittys took off in sixes at twenty-minute intervals having been allocated the target area of Rover David and a secondary target if he did not call for support during that particular twenty minutes. Each pilot had a copy of the gridded map. The leader would patrol the primary area for twenty minutes calling up Rover David to ask if he had a target. If he had, then it was not only identified on the gridded map but sighted on the ground by the leader. He and his No 2 would then dive-bomb the particular target, which would be, say, a wood or farmhouse. Everyone watched the target to see how near the bombs fell. For the next two to go down, Rover David could correct the initial bombing by an instruction such as "place your bombs 100 yards (91 m) to the north-east of the first bomb bursts" and so on. Then the Kittys could be requested to strafe a particular area. In this way the Army could be said to be using our Kittys as 'Air Artillery', with the service always available as we queued up to cover the area in twenty minute slots. Hence the name 'Cab-Rank'.

If Rover David had no target in that particular twenty minutes, then our Kittys could proceed to the secondary target and bomb and strafe without further reference to him. It could be very motivating to be told by David that the attack had been exactly right – much jubilation. If our bombs were not right or even too near David himself, then his comments could be unprintable! The truth was that our dive-bombing had an element of luck and was therefore not always accurate. The Cab-Rank system we perfected was much used later, on the Normandy invasion of mainland Europe.

On 2 November we carried out one such op when the primary target was a wooded area. Rover wanted us to dive-bomb this target 200 yards (183 m) south of San Salvo. The first two down, with two 250 pounders (113 kg) each, were quite accurate so he told us to put the rest of our bombs as near as possible to the first bursts. My bombs were not so good but most were in the target area. There was no opposition and the whole trip took only fifty minutes. Rover was very pleased.

Our Army would help us as much as possible by firing at the enemy as we came down to bomb, with the effect of concentrating the enemy mind on ground attack rather than firing their guns up at us. A very rewarding team spirit grew between the two services, each with a great respect for the other's efforts. To further this understanding, a policy of exchanging positions was begun. An Army officer would be sent to live with the squadron for a few days, then a pilot would be sent to a forward Army position. We both agreed that we would rather do our own job! I was not looking forward to my turn to go.

Later in November we went on another Rover trip, but didn't have a target so we went on to the secondary near Adriano – a road and railway crossing. There was no opposition to our attack, probably because the Jerries were too busy shooting at our Army for we could see a terrific artillery battle going on below with flashes from both sides. Our bombing was fair and probably closed the crossing for the time being at least.

From this time onwards we flew many road and rail interdiction flights as part of the Allied strategy of slowing down or stopping all communications that may help the Jerries. Several trips were against the railway system. The terrain in the Apennines was such that railways crossed hundreds of bridges and went through many tunnels.

We did enjoy having a go at a railway engine. If caught right, which wasn't very often, it would cause a cloud of steam, smoke and flames.

On one such trip we spied a train entering a tunnel. We waited for it to come out the other end but they were too crafty for that. So we decided to have a go at sealing it in. Our bottom six dive-bombed the entrance and it caved in nicely. I went down with the top six to block the exit. We had a grim sense of humour here. Our bombs fell all around the tunnel and on the track, so I think the enemy had some heavy repair work to do to get the train out again!

Our interdiction work took us to many bridges to be blown up. It was difficult to know what results we had achieved when so many of our bombs did not hit the bridge directly, so we did not claim much success. However, as our Army moved forward, they reported more successes for us than we had realized.

Foggia Main and other satellites were now occupied by the USAAF. Foggia completed a ring of bases around Germany from all of which bombers could reach that country. There was also a squadron of American Thunderbolts operating from Foggia main. Their discipline was not up to our standard. For example, we maintained very tight radio silence and, when we did have to speak, were very careful not to give away any information that the enemy could use to its advantage. After all we had our own 'Y' Service working well, so no doubt the Jerries were doing something roughly similar. Imagine our chagrin one day to hear an American voice on the R/T saying clearly:

"Hello Bubbly Tower. Hello Bubbly Tower. Flight of six Thunderbolts coming in over Foggia to land now".

In one sentence that intrepid aviator had given away:

1) his call sign

2) the type of aircraft he was flying

3) the aerodrome from which he was operating and

4) the number of aircraft in a flight!

We listened to quite a lot of American pilot's chat – mostly it was flowery and amusing. The enemy linguists listening were no doubt enjoying it too.

On 12 November, we were off to Yugoslavia anti-shipping again. We flew around the island of Braki and over Supator harbour but found no target so we returned to base. On the 19th I saw Flying Officer 'Hawk-Eye' Wilkinson shot down over Ripa. He baled out and it was hoped he would survive. Later we learned that he was a POW. We called him 'Hawk-Eye' because, he claimed, he was the first to see any enemy aircraft approach.

On the 21st we bombed troop concentrations south-east. of Mozzadragno. The frightening aspect of this trip was an intense 'box' barrage of 88 mm from around Lanchiano. I hadn't seen this form of ack-ack defence since mixing with our own Navy off Pantelleria. I fired my guns on the way down in the hope of putting off the Jerry gunners but I don't think it made any difference.

On the last day of the month I flew a close army support six with Rover; another Cab-Rank trip, this time to some houses at a roadside. Again we were unopposed probably because the Jerries were busy returning our Army's fire. We Sharks and other Kitty squadrons were reckoned, by the Army, to have broken up an enemy counter-attack – very rewarding. I had done two Cab-Rank ops that day. Again, that day, 2nd Lieutenant Hanreck of the SAAF flew his first op with us in the top six. As he attempted to dive he was hit. I saw him complete his dive and then glide to the coast and land on a beach. I stayed with him so I could report what had happened. I last saw him with a rowing boat approaching. I never did hear of him again but he probably became a POW. It didn't seem fair at any time, let alone when it was his very first op! I wasn't on this particular op, but in early December we lost two Kittys on the same day, both hit by flak in the radiator. Eventually both pilots got back to the squadron. 'Tex' Gray was one of them. He really was an American from Texas. There will be more about him later. This day his engine seized up while over enemy territory. He managed to glide to the right side of the bomb line and force land.

The other was 'Happy' Ahern who force-landed on our side and got a lift back to the squadron.

About this time Jackie Darwen was posthumously awarded the DSO.

My Kitty 'Z', FR388, was due for a major overhaul so I flew in 'H' in December. I didn't like it very much. Each aeroplane had its different little peculiarities. I can't say why but I was just not comfortable in it. December was a quiet month for flying due to the weather and so we set about the serious business of enjoying Christmas as much as possible under the circumstances.

CHAPTER SEVENTEEN

THE IRISH FIRING SQUAD

Johnnie Burcham was honorary messing officer and several of us helped him on his purchasing trips around the local countryside. One such trip was in a 3-ton truck up into the mountainous 'spur' of Italy. We traversed a myriad of hairpin bends on this journey, bringing back a load of cauliflowers and a pig, all paid for in British Occupation Currency. On another outing there was great excitement buying a bullock. Much bargaining took place. Our Corporal cook was also a qualified butcher. He advised us that running down a pig to get one for nothing, was not going to be good value because the meat would be too bruised. Just an idea! Another time twenty turkeys were bought. All this livestock made the old farmhouse come alive. There was no problem with the pig or turkeys but the bullock was very frisky and it was too soon to slaughter it so we had to tie it up in the farmyard. It must have been a bit nervous for the next day it broke loose and rampaged among the tents causing some broken guy ropes and much annoyance. We chased after it but it was too fast for us, galloping into the middle of the landing ground. Now it was the turn of the CO to get nervous, worrying of the possibility of broken Kittys trying to land and take off. He felt the bullock could hinder the war effort and ordered it to be disposed of immediately.

Tex Gray had found a horse to ride. Where he got it from no one seemed to know but he got a rope to use as a lasso and set out in proper Texan style after the bullock. All we could think of was to use our firearms. We got all the pistols and rifles we could and set off in all directions to the landing ground. We had surrounded the bullock but the problem remained like an Irish Firing Squad with us all shooting each other instead of the bull! Bullets whistled all around. Eventually, when Tex was not in the way someone got in a good shot to the bullock's head and it slumped to the ground. The Corporal was quickly on the scene and after much humping across the ground, the bullock was removed to the cookhouse tent and properly slaughtered. We all stood around watching the butcher at work until he got to inserting a bit of wire through the bullet hole into its brain and twiddling it around till the dead bullock stopped twitching. It made me feel a bit poorly but didn't stop me enjoying the meat when it was roasted and served. This fresh meat was a great treat for us having been on bully beef or Spam for many months.

The Engineering Officer was determined we should all be warm and kept piling timber on the fire under the old chimney. We called him a pyromaniac. Shortly he realized that the chimney breast was built of timber as well as stone, because smoke and flames came belching out the top as it caught fire. A chain gang of buckets up the roof and water down the chimney was eventually the answer. After cleaning up the mess we relit the fire on a more modest scale.

Christmas Day arrived with a plentiful supply of food to be washed down with Chianti and other local wines. We followed the RAF tradition, so the officers and pilots served a good dinner to the NCOs and men, commencing with Peter the CO and Taffy the Adjutant carrying on a plate the decorated pig's head resplendent with apple in its mouth, to great cheers. The CO made a speech and by about four o'clock in the afternoon most retired to their tents to sleep it off. For a couple of days we could put on one side thoughts of the future and what it had in store for us.

We had tremendous respect for the ground staff. They worked all hours and often in very uncomfortable and difficult conditions, sometimes right through the night to see our Kittys were as serviceable as humanly possible. The messing staff performed miracles with the sometimes very meagre and dull provisions available. We all worked as a team to do our bit for what we believed in to defeat the Jerries who we had come to hate for all they stood for. The ground staff were always waiting for our return from ops, counting the Kittys as they came in to land and often in tears for a missing pilot. They were one hundred percent loyal. My fitter Nick was always there to help undo my straps and parachute harness and in return I gave him a quick resume of what had happened on that particular op. There were successes and disappointments alike.

The CO and Adjutant with the decoration for the Christmas table, 'I ain't got no body'

'Nick' Nicholas, the fitter with 'Z - Zephyr Breezes' that he looked after so well

The armourers handled the bombs and machine gun belts most expertly and with great aplomb. I remember seeing them tip 1,000 lb (453 kg) bombs out of a 3-tonner truck on to the ground with a great thump – no real danger as the experts knew, but it did make me wince especially when, one day, a 1,000 lb bomb burst open when it thumped on the ground and it had to be disposed of. Perhaps they were more careful after that!

January, despite the weather, was a busy month for the Shark Squadron. I personally flew seventeen operational sorties. Our work was varied; much of it close army support in central Italy despite snow on the ground, interspersed with anti-shipping trips to Yugoslavia.

On the 2nd we bombed and strafed gun positions at Miglianico. Despite 40 mm and 20 mm ack-ack all got back safely. There were similar trips in Italy on the 3rd and 4th. Then on the 7th I led the top six to shipping in Makarska harbour in Yugoslavia. We each carried a 500 lb (226 kg) bomb under the fuselage and 40 pounders (18 kg) under the wings. This time we found two schooners and some smaller ships and bombed successfully leaving one schooner listing and the other with at least some damage. This shipping was supplying Jerry troops in their fight with General Tito and the partisans in Yugoslavia.

It was a good feeling, leading the top six Kittys. I had the responsibility of positioning the six to enable us all to get a good aim on the target. Had to pull up to the right height and position so the other five could re-formate on me and join up with the other flight. We had some light ack-ack but all returned safely after an hour and fifty minutes in the air.

We had the same sort of trip to Yugoslavia on each of the next two days. We found a large oil tank and, despite bombing and strafing, it just would not burn. I reckon it was empty. On this trip 2nd Lieutenant Sharp called up to say he had lost rudder control completely in intense Breda fire. I had to shepherd him back across the Adriatic. He didn't quite make the landing ground but had to force-land about five miles short. His Kitty was a write-off but he survived to get back to Melini.

On the 14th we found a 1,000-ton cargo ship in Sibenik harbour and, despite some small arms fire, left it burning. We went to strafe a small schooner and riddled it with bullets till it sank. It didn't have a chance against twelve Kittys. On the 18th, we went again to Yugoslavia where the first six got a direct hit on a 1,000-ton ship. Myself and my No 2 dived separately to silence six 40 mm guns, firing from an emplacement, that were endangering the whole squadron. Both 500 pounders (225 kg) landed among them and they stopped firing.

I flew two close army support sorties next with some success and some disappointments because of inaccurate bombing. On the 21st, I went on a long trip to Yugoslavia in my Kitty 'Z'. Again the target was shipping, this time in Ploca harbour. Again I went off to silence some 40mm gun positions. I was just going in for a second strafing run when there was a thump and the stick was nearly jerked out of my hand. I pulled up to find a 40mm hole clean through the left aileron. I was just lucky that the shell had gone through without exploding. 'Z' felt slightly different on aileron control, otherwise all was well. I came back feeling slightly chastened. I had been in the air two hours and fifteen minutes without a long range tank.

On the 22nd, I was back on armed recce over the Avezzano–Popoli area. There was much Jerry MT on the roads but it was heavily defended with intense and accurate Breda fire. I dropped two 250 pounders (113 kg) with anti-personnel rods and must have done some damage with my bombs. Only one strafing run was wise in these conditions. I claimed four MT destroyed.

The last trip of the month was to be well remembered for the rest of my life without the need of my diary or log book to remind me. We set off on an armed recce of six, each with only a long range belly tank and the machine guns fully loaded, of course. The target was a large convoy of Jerry MT on the roads between Avezzano, Arce and Soru. We were only just approaching the area when a terrific barrage of ack-ack came up at us. As it says in my logbook: "Hadn't seen anything like it since the Messina Straits". As it began to burst among us, my No 2 broke formation and went off leaving me without support. The target was a specific one. The Army wanted these convoys attacked so there was no question of not going on because of heavy opposition.

Eighty-eight millimetre flak was bursting all around, black and so close I could see the bright red centres, buffeting my Kitty 'W'. Then came a voice on the R/T screaming at me: "Green 1, your belly tank is on fire! Drop it quick – for God's sake listen! Drop your belly tank!" There was a lot of black smoke around. I didn't wait to find out whether it was

88 mm or my tank on fire, so I jettisoned it quickly. The smoke cleared. I could now see much transport on the roads beneath, so I started to go down to strafe with the rest of the flight. I only did one run, leaving two trucks on fire, then decided to find my way back home in case I ran out of petrol without my long range tank. The rest of the flight went on to further strafing.

I felt very lonely aiming for base all on my own and furious that my No 2 had let me down. I returned to base over Gaeta on the west coast as the quickest route to our side of the bomb line, so that, if I did have to bale out or force land, at least it would be over our own territory. I had some 88 mm thrown up at me over Gaeta and began to wonder if I had come the best way. I saw some Jerry MT on the road and went down to strafe them, thinking it was on my way home and that I wouldn't use much more petrol. On pulling the gun trigger there was only the pathetic sound of one gun firing. I pulled up and set the throttle for maximum fuel saving and continued back to base, very conscious that I was a prime target for any enemy fighter who might spot me. The fuel gauge was reading zero as I came in over Melini. I slipped off some height and landed quickly but carefully. I didn't want to risk going round again with so little petrol. Nick sat on the wing tip to guide me in to the right dispersal point. I climbed out but had a job to keep standing, my knees were so wobbly.

I reported to the IO, then went back with Nick to see what damage there was to 'W'. Under the fuselage great singe marks were clearly to be seen. Also shrapnel had damaged five of the guns, preventing them firing. I had never heard of a belly tank catching fire without blowing up and get looks of disbelief when I tell the tale. However several colleagues saw it on fire and the entry is in my logbook and signed by the then CO, Peter Illingworth.

Only four more Kittys got back from that trip. The sixth was hit and the pilot had to bale out over that German convoy; most unfortunate to say the least. When they were back I had to have a private word with two of them. First the No 2 who had chickened out. I had a private word. His excuse was that he felt he could find a safer way to the target than through the middle of the ack-ack. I didn't believe him and told him what I thought of him in unrepeatable language and made a mental note never to have him as my No 2 again. Secondly, I gave a big thank you to the pilot who had seen my belly tank burning and had shouted the warning.

About this time an officer had travelled over the Apennines to Naples to see what that great city had to offer and had come back having rented a flat overlooking the bay for the pilots and officers to enjoy when we had a break and could borrow some transport. There will be more about this later.

Now January 1944 was behind me. I had flown ninety-six operational sorties, had led the top six on several occasions and began to feel I might survive to complete my tour of operations which was reckoned to be about 120 ops. Most of us had been awarded the Africa Star with Clasp. We were especially proud of the clasp, which indicated that we had fought with the Desert Air Force alongside the 8th Army – the 'Desert Rats'.

Our Army had sent a sea-borne force to invade the mainland well north of Naples, at Anzio, in an attempt to open up the fighting and in the hope of pushing faster north. Now we flew our aircraft to a landing ground on the beach further north at Cutella near the town of Vasto on the east coast.

CHAPTER EIGHTEEN

LACK OF MORAL FIBRE

Cutella was a landing strip among the sand dunes between the beach and the railway line a few yards south east of the river Trigno. It was a very cramped area and all our tents, huts and equipment were compacted around the PSP strip. It was quite wide enough for us to take off in pairs. I think it was about 1,000 yards long (914 m) plus a few extra yards of flat sandy area beyond the steel planking. We didn't worry too much about the wind direction, taking off from the dispersal area and landing back towards it. Through daylight hours there was a number of pilots at 'readiness'. The CO had put our names on the 'Gaggle Board' to indicate the positions we were to maintain in the formation. Before taking off we were briefed by the IO as to where the bomb-line was on that day, any known ack-ack positions and the details of the target. This was all done in a matter of minutes and we could be airborne in a quarter of an hour or so. The leader would map-read to the target area. If the weather conditions were such that this was impossible then it meant we couldn't do our job anyway, so we didn't go.

For months and months we had been promised that prefabricated wooden huts were on the way, to improve our living conditions. Rumour had it that they were on the way from England but that the walls had been loaded on one ship and all the roofs on another. Not many ships survived the journey through the Med and it was said that there was a plentiful supply of roofs but no walls to hold them up! However, at Cutella, we were supplied with one corrugated iron Nissen hut. This became the pilots' and officers' lounge/bar. A separate tent for eating was arranged. The problem was that we were cold. We set about solving this with a marvellous heating system. We stood an empty 40 gallon (181 ltr) drum on bricks in the middle of the hut and cut an air inlet and a hole for a chimney, which pilot Ken Stokes made out of about thirty 2 gallon (9 ltr) cans beaten into shape. Outside we stood a 90 gallon (409 ltr) belly tank of petrol on trestles with a small bore pipe running through the wall of the hut and into the 40 gallon drum. Very simple. We just turned on a tap carefully so that the petrol dripped into the floor of the drum. Lighting the petrol was a bit hairy but after a few minor explosions we got the petrol dripping just right to heat up the drum to a suitable temperature.

The author swinging the charcoal fire.
Cutella, February 1944

Nissen hut at Cutella, February 1944. Note the innovative chimney

The Americans had the same idea and, on a visit back to Foggia Main, we saw a whole tented camp, each with its own 'furnace' burning away the petrol so that there was a permanent haze of petrol smoke over the whole camp! Trust the Yanks to do everything bigger! For our tents we had a more economical method of heating. There was a plentiful supply of charcoal locally so we punched holes in an empty potato tin and fitted wire for swinging it around. We filled with charcoal and just a modicum of petrol to set it alight and we had a useful little brazier to heat our tent and to cook a little extra food during small parties therein. 'Swinging the charcoal' to make our heaters burn brightly became a common sight in the encampment.

At the end of our Nissen hut was a bar manned at nightfall by Corporal Brown for when ops were over for the day. We had a radio, of course, as well as a gramophone with the usual selection of Glenn Miller and other pop records of the time. Vera Lynn was our favourite and she did a request programme. I wrote to her and at Cutella heard her say "The next

number is for Bert Horden and the boys of 112 Squadron". She was right
– we were boys really.

One-One-Two had the airstrip to itself, apart from an Air-Sea
Rescue flight consisting of one Walrus amphibian, its pilot and ground
crew. We had our ambulance always at the ready at the side of the strip,
with its engine running and the Squadron MO in the passenger seat, whenever we took off or landed. It was not often needed but was a comforting
sight.

An Air Sea Rescue Supermarine Walrus at Cutella, March 1944

We took off in pairs and circled around the strip at least once to
allow all aircraft to catch up and formate. For landing we dropped back
from the formation, into echelon starboard, then into line astern to come
in singly. From Cutella we took off sometimes with up to 2,000 lbs (907
kg) total bomb load. This was not easy. It called for full flaps and holding
brakes full-on till the Kitty was reared up like a horse ready to go. On
releasing the brakes the aircraft leaped forward for, hopefully, a short take

off. On one occasion at Cutella, I was taking off in formation with another Kitty when it failed to get more than a few feet off the ground and at the end of the metal strip sank back onto the ground, ploughing through several tents before coming to rest – and that with its wheels nearly retracted and a 1,000 lb (453 kg) bomb under it! I was in the air myself but all on the ground must have put their fingers in ears in case the bomb went off. Miraculously no-one was hurt but the tents were relocated quite quickly.

With this heavy bomb load, our Kittys had to circle around for a while to gain sufficient height to fly over the mountains of Frentani, the two main peaks of which formed a 'saddle'. With 1,500 lbs (680 kg) bomb load we found we could just scrape over the saddle after one circuit of the airstrip. This we did, not realizing that the bomb line was this side of the saddle. Jerry must have gone to great lengths to drag a 20mm gun up into the mountains. He would think it worthwhile because it opened fire one day as 112 Squadron was struggling a few hundred feet above and shot down one of our Kittys in flames. It must have been an easy target. I wasn't on that trip myself but we all felt deep regret that we hadn't realized the danger and consequently lost a pilot. He did not survive.

Eight miles north up the coast was a blown-up lighthouse at Penna Point. In the buildings attached was accommodated our 'Y' Service and also our Controller whose call sign was 'Commander', working closely together. Commander could hear all that was said on our R/T and he could call us up to warn of enemy aircraft in the area. If the 'Y' Service heard Jerry pilots talking, saying for example, six Kittyhawks at 12 o'clock below, then he would call us up and say "Enemy aircraft at 6 o'clock above and they have just spotted you". This service really was that good on many occasions. I don't know if Jerry had such a good service working for him or not. Commander could also give us a course to steer for base should it become necessary.

We moved to Cutella in early February 1944 and the next day I was out bombing a factory building near Chieti. The Baltimores and Thunderbolts also bombed. There was a huge explosion at the target. The 88mm ack-ack was intense and accurate and two of our Kittys collected flak holes, but survived. Chieti became a dirty word among us pilots, it was so heavily defended.

Bad weather prevented us flying for a few days but on the 8th we had an unusual armed recce. Just south of Sara we found a huge Jerry convoy of MT. It was unusual because it was undefended. We dive-bombed along the road to ensure best results. We could achieve greater accuracy this way than at 90% to the road. This time, undisturbed by flak, the results were good and all bombs fell on or near the targets. As there were no repercussions, we went down to strafe. I was leading the top six, impatiently waiting our turn in case the Jerries found some guns to fire at us. I went down to strafe six times according to my log book. I remember seeing a petrol bowser among the lorries on the road and having a go at it. Eventually it blew up in flames reaching high into the air. We all got back safely this time.

Again bad weather prevented us operating and the forecast for the next few days was so bad that the CO allowed a few of us to go to Naples to enjoy the squadron flat. The best part of the outing was the journey over the Appian way and back. It was not very comfortable as I spent most of the time in the back of the 13-cwt truck bouncing along the rough roads, but the view was most refreshing – lovely countryside partly swathed in mist, little villages perched atop of hills, peasants with donkey carts on the road. I felt we were seeing the real southern Italy.

The flat was several storeys up by lift in an apartment block on the sea front overlooking the bay. There was a magnificent view of the Bay of Naples with Vesuvius gently belching little clouds that the wind drifted away. Some of the locals provided us with a superb meal, including squid and other Mediterranean delights I had never tasted before. During daytime we explored the city centre looking for souvenirs. Some of the shops were beginning to open now that the fighting had moved north. We made friends with the owner of a large drapery store on the Via Roma, and his family. They took us to see the sights we might otherwise have missed. The city was undamaged and we were glad that these Italians were no longer our enemies.

These few days sped by and, on our return to the Squadron, it was sad to hear of another lost pilot, especially as it was not due to enemy action this time. Flight Sergeant Doug Holmes took his Kitty up just for a simple air test and was never seen again. We presumed he had become lost in the heavy clouds. A search was made to no effect. We did learn, however, about this time that 'Hawk-Eye' Wilkinson was a POW.

On the 22nd I was off again across the Adriatic to Yugoslavia to attack shipping. As we approached the target area, Tex Gray announced over the R/T that his engine was getting rough. As was the custom, someone had to go back with him in case he didn't get all the way back to base. I went with him, flying in echelon starboard. It must have seemed an age to Tex with his engine juddering but we made it back to base. His engine bearings had gone leaving a big job for the ground staff to fit a new engine.

Next day six of us flew again to Yugoslavia. In Zadar harbour we found some barges and other assorted shipping, and dive-bombed. Someone's bomb got a direct hit on a barge, which blew up. It must have been loaded with ammunition for the Jerries. As there was only light opposition we strafed the other shipping. I spotted a W/T station nearby so made a quick burst of fire at it before re-forming for the flight back to base.

On the 24th we attempted to climb up over the saddle in an effort to carry out an armed recce of the Arce area but the cloud-base was low in this mountainous area and our controls started to freeze up, so we had to turn back to base with our bombs.

You will have noticed that I haven't referred to any enemy aircraft lately. We Allies now had air-superiority and when we did see enemy aircraft in the distance they usually disappeared rather then engage in dog-fights. Despite this, sometimes we were escorted to a target by Spitfires, just in case.

On the 27th we were ordered to destroy Tortoeto railway station. I was Blue 1, leading the top six, and we were escorted by a couple of Spits from 7 SAAF Wing. As we approached the target area a load of 88 mm flak came up at us. I saw Black 2 leave the formation. I knew he was on his first op with the Squadron, so called him up on the R/T to see what was the matter – no reply. We pressed on to the target where we dive-bombed the station and marshalling yard. There was some ack-ack but not as bad as usual over that area and, apart from the 'new boy', all got back safely.

That evening a signal was received by the Adjutant to advise us that one of our Kittyhawks had landed at Capo di Chini Airport at Naples. This turned out to be our 'new boy' who said his engine was running rough. The CO told him to stay there for the moment and then instructed me to go and sort it out. Next day I got a lift from Foggia Main to Naples Airport in an

American DC-3, flown by a man with the lovely name of Captain Elber B Hiram. He said "Sure, come and be my second pilot". Naples Airport was being used by a large variety of Air Force Units: English Spitfires, American bombers, South African medium bombers and so on.

I spotted the Shark Kitty and found our 'new boy'. He seemed very nervous so I told him to wait while I checked the engine of his Kitty. The engine ran up all right on the ground so I took it off for a test flight. He made me feel nervous too as this was my first attempt as a 'test pilot' – however all was perfectly good.

The Americans were most hospitable and 'new boy' and I sat down to a breakfast. I seem to remember it was bacon, hash browns and maple syrup – what a combination! I had a long talk with our 'new boy' and eventually he broke down in tears admitting that he was just plain scared. I told him I was too. I sent him back to Cutella in his Kitty while I got a lift back in a B-17 Flying Fortress. Again, I was designated second pilot. When I got back I had to advise the CO that our 'new boy' was 'just not up to it'. The CO posted him away immediately as suffering from LMF and I never heard of him again. He was, no doubt, stripped of his pilot's wings.

A few days later a P-51 Mustang Fighter arrived for us to evaluate, for it was proposed that we convert on to these more advanced fighters.

On 28 February I had a thirty-five minute flight in this Mustang 1A. I had got so used to a Kitty feeling like an extension of my arms and legs that the Mustang seemed strange and not so comfortable. However, its performance was a big improvement and after a few hours flying I believe I would have liked it very much. In the event I was not to fly one again.

The Squadron had only one concern at converting to Mustangs: would the Shark Mouth look good on it? This Shark insignia had become such an important part of our image that we tried to change our Egyptian Cat badge for a Shark but without success. Instead, some artistic ground staff designed a 'Diving Shark' design to paint onto the squadron MT. It was also painted on the front of the bar!

The first Mustang. April 1944

CHAPTER NINETEEN

TEX GRAY AND LIFE IN THE ARMY

Tex Gray was a tall American with an untidy mop of ginger hair. He really was from Texas and became the Squadron 'character'. Hearing that there was a war on and wanting some of the action, he joined the RCAF, earned his wings and found his way to Cairo. As the Americans were now officially in the war, Tex could have opted to be transferred to the USAAF but preferred to stay, calling his countrymen "Those goddam Yanks". From Cairo he thumbed a lift to 239 Wing and persuaded the Groupy to let him fly with our Shark Squadron.

Two pilots at ablutions: left Tex Gray and right, Lt. Pinky. February 1944

He was a good pilot but preferred to 'do his own thing' and often disappeared from formation to pick a fight with his own Jerry target at deck level. Despite this he always turned up back at the Squadron base, usually late and short of petrol. Because of his unique national status and the fact that he had never been officially posted to the Squadron, he was the only one of us not to have to conform to Squadron discipline. He usually found a horse to ride and with his Texan skill occasionally roped in a 'steer' to provide the pilots mess with some juicy steaks. He was still on the Squadron when I left but I heard that he completed his tour of ops with many extra sorties before being sent on his way by the CO.

Towards the end of February we set off, Tex included, to dive-bomb in support of the Anzio bridgehead. Our twelve Kittys dive-bombed enemy positions in some houses and some success was observed. This time we were subjected to very intense Breda gun-fire as well as small arms fire as we pulled out of the dive. Tex Gray was hit and he had to force land rather quickly near La Villa, fortunately on the right side of the bomb line. I circled around at a respectful distance until I saw Tex leave his Kitty and run away, then I returned to base. Tex himself had some flak splinters in his left leg. His report to the IO on his return was a masterpiece. He said he had to force-land "due to increased wing loading imposed by a quantity of flak in his left leg". On landing he said "The Kittyhawk began to hiss and crackle in an unpleasant manner and there was a smell as of urinating on a hot stove!" He exited from his Kitty "like a champagne cork out of the bottle" and, realizing that he had landed in a mine field, raced across it in about "ten seconds flat". This journey took about two hours for those who approached the aircraft through the mines later!

On 2 March, armed with a 1,000 lb (453 kg) bomb, we went to roads south-east of Rome to attack MT. Again there was some 88 mm flak and small arms fire as we pulled out of the dive. I claimed two lorries destroyed and four damaged. The next trip was to a similar target but on this one I took time out to circle my Flight over Rome and the river Tiber. Both sides of the conflict had agreed not to bomb Rome as one of the world's architectural treasure troves, so we were careful just to have a look. It was quite an experience to look down on the great and beautiful city for the first time. The trip took two hours and ten minutes with no belly tanks so we were all short of petrol. Aussie pilot Bernie Peters ran out of petrol in the circuit and he had to come in on a crackling engine and dead stick. He just made it nicely. This was fortunate or I might have been in trouble for messing about over Rome!

I led the top six on a few trips to Yugoslavia on anti-shipping recces. Once we had to return due to bad weather. In mid-March I found myself acting as 'test-pilot' again. This time the CO sent me by road to Foggia Main to test and deliver a Kitty to the squadron. I got there late in the evening and the only place to sleep was in the local RAF hospital at the end of a long ward, otherwise full of injured airmen. I got to sleep despite the moaning and groaning and was up before dawn and out to the airfield to collect the Kitty. I took off into the steely-grey dawn, did my test and flew on back to Cutella. The same day I led the top six to Monte Cassino to dive-bomb Jerry troops in the area. This time, most bombs were good despite some accurate 40 mm flak.

Other trips were to Yugoslavia to bomb and strafe shipping. We didn't get shot at by the dreaded 88 mm on these shipping runs, only 40mm and 20mm. Now we started on some anti-shipping sorties up the east coast of Italy even further north than Ancona.

On the 27th I had to fly to Aquila leading the top six to demolish Antrodoca viaduct. Our 500 lb (226 kg) bombs dropped on the railway lines but the bridge seemed to remain intact. We had just pulled out of our dive when we spotted a Fieseler Storch just coming in to land at Aquila airfield. The Jerry pilot must have felt dreadful with twelve Kittyhawks all bearing down on him anxious to claim a 'kill'. In the event, the Storch wheels were just touching the grass when our bullets struck home. The Storch did a bouncy landing, the pilot leapt out and ran across the grass while his aircraft burst into flames. The pilot fell to the ground and lay still. Whether he was hit or just lying doggo in the hopes that we stopped shooting, we shall never know. Myself and Ken Stokes went around for another strafing run because we had spotted a Macchi 202 fighter under the trees with some MT. We left the Macchi damaged and the MT burning. And so we went back to base without loss. It was much more satisfactory shooting at Jerry aircraft than at MT, although both were exciting.

About this time my friend Johnnie Burcham was shot down in central Italy. His engine seized up and he had to make a forced landing in the flat irrigated area south east of Avezzano in enemy territory. I wasn't on that trip myself but stood counting the Kittys back home as they came in to land. I kept losing friends; now it was my best friend. I quizzed all on the trip with some relief to hear they had seen Johnnie land and run away from his aircraft. I had the wild idea that I could go and pick him up and bring him back. I realised I couldn't go in a Kitty but the AOC had a captured Fieseler Storch which was ideal for a short landing and take off. I pleaded with the CO, Peter Illingworth, who was good enough to put through a call to Group Headquarters. He was only being kind, seeing my distress, and, of course, the answer was "Sorry, no". I collected up Johnnie's belongings from his tent and hoped to take them back, one day, to the UK and thence to his mother. Later we heard that he was a POW.

Another pilot returned badly shot up from this trip and had to belly-land on the beach near to base. His wheels would not come down and landing on the steel planking would have been disastrous. He made a super landing under the circumstances, close enough to our ground-staff repair team. We told him he should have landed directly on to the trestles to save lifting gear ! I don't think he found it funny at the time.

I was getting a bit depressed with the loss of so many friends – and was more scared than I had been.

It became my turn to visit the Army, on the exchange basis mentioned earlier, so I set off in a truck heading northwards, driven by an army Captain who had just spent a few easy days watching our Kittyhawks take off and land and getting plastered each evening in our Nissen hut. He still said he preferred his job to ours. I never have understood this because my three days with the army were cold, wet and uncomfortable. The 1st Airborne Division platoon that I visited was positioned in an old draughty, tumbledown farmhouse overlooking a valley somewhere around Ortona. The food was quite good – tinned beef stew and that sort of thing – but did not taste as good out of a billycan as off a proper plate. Every few hours the Jerries opened fire with their 88 mm gunfire – here we go again! The farmhouse shook and bits of plaster fell into our stew, just as in an American war film. I was quite frightened – I wanted to hide under the table or somewhere – but the soldiers took absolutely no notice at all. They had learned to live with it. Our guns replied from behind us every now and again. I slept on a palliasse on the floor. The first night was reasonably quiet but on the second day the Sergeant in charge began planning a patrol to be sent out that night. They took it for granted that I would like to go to see some action. I never felt less like a 'night out' in my life! A Captain came and asked if I was finding it interesting. I had to say "Yes" out of politeness. He was a cheerful chap and a lot of banter was exchanged between him and the NCOs. I admired their sense of humour enormously. More shell fire – more dust and plaster. I was issued with a rifle which I assured the Sergeant I could use, thanks to my Home Guard training. He explained that the objective was to discover the strength and exact positions of Jerries encamped around derelict houses about half a mile away. He said he hoped we wouldn't get into a shooting match but must be ready to defend ourselves. I couldn't have agreed with him more.

As evening approached I became very apprehensive. However, at dusk the Captain turned up again and said the patrol was off! I didn't know what to say to this. I didn't want them to think I was chicken – even if I was. I felt like cheering and making whoopee – in the end I tried to look philosophical, as they were. I played poker in the light of torches – couldn't concentrate – lost a little money, much to the Army's delight. Next morning I crept away from the farmhouse to where a truck was waiting and bounced back along the track and roads leading to Cutella – with great relief and a terrific admiration for the British Army.

Squadron Leader Peter Illingworth was shot down while strafing some E-boats around the island of Ciovo in Yugoslavia. He was last seen with glycol streaming from his radiator as he headed for the mainland to try a forced landing. One of the Flight Commanders took over the Squadron temporarily.

On 29 March I brought back a small piece of a German truck from a trip to destroy another bridge. We carried a 500 pounder (226 kg) under the fuselage as well as 40 pounders (18 kg) under the wings. We left the bridge slightly damaged. I went down to take a close look at the bridge to assess the situation – perhaps not a wise thing to do. However there was only slight 20 mm fire from a gun on a railway truck. We strafed these trucks and must have damaged them severely although they didn't burn. We silenced the gun. I saw two very large German looking juggernauts on a road nearby and went to strafe one of them. Must have been packed with explosives because it blew up in my gunsight with a mighty roar and a column of smoke rising well above a 1,000 ft (304 m) which I had to fly through. Fortunately, it was my first burst of fire that set off the explosion and I had time to take some evasive action. If I had continued down for a second burst, I reckon I would have been brought down by the explosion itself. As it was, I felt it rock my Kitty 'Z' and when I got back to base Nick proudly showed me what he had found embedded in the wing. It was a metal bracket with splinters of wood attached, obviously a part of the demolished Jerry juggernaut. I let him keep it as a souvenir.

During the last few days of March we were busy on sorties to bomb bridges, hopefully to paralyse Jerry communications – mostly routine trips. Sometimes there was a bit of flak to contend with. Sometimes we damaged a bridge – often not knowing the result. Rarely did we see a bridge completely demolished by our bombs. It really needed the medium bombers to do that and they were busy also at this time, having a go.

Our new CO was Squadron Leader Watts, an Aussie from 3 RAAF Squadron on our Wing, so he understood our work very well.

About this time we had a very unhappy occurrence. Let me set the scene from the air. The imaginary bomb-line I have talked about already was just a line on a map in the IO's truck/office. You would think there was no such line on the ground. This is true. However, one could see from the air which was our side and which was Jerry's by the number of MT visible on the roads and the masses of aircraft around landing grounds on our side. Our air superiority was such that the Jerries had to hide their aircraft under trees and move their MT, tanks, etc at night, so the roads and airfields looked deserted from the air in the daytime – their side of the bomb-line. It seemed inexcusable then that one bright sunny morning two USAAF P-38 Lightnings suddenly dived down over Cutella strip full of aircraft and began to strafe. There was nothing else to do but lie flat on the ground and pray. After two runs at us the Americans flew away south. We stood up to assess the damage. The Walrus amphibian air-sea rescue aircraft had been damaged and its RAF pilot who was working on it at the time was shot and killed. In addition several of our Kittyhawks were damaged. We learned later that the two US pilots had been sent back to the States in disgrace. I am not sure this was a punishment. At least they got back to their families and safety! A stupid mistake like this can be horrific in wartime.

CHAPTER TWENTY

FASCIST HQ – MACERATA

Our 'Y' Service at Penna Point was in touch with Italian partisans operating against the Germans and Fascist Italian collaborators around Macerata much further north. They learnt that senior German officers were to meet in Macerata in the Town Hall on the piazza at 11 am in the morning of 3 April 1944 with Fascist leaders from all around the area. It was deemed to be such an important meeting that a big security operation had been initiated involving German troops from the nearby barracks. The partisans were excited to have learned of this secret meeting and informed the Allied 'Y' Service at once. When our AOC (Air Officer Commanding) heard of this interesting bit of intelligence he decided to support the partisans by mounting an RAF operation against the town hall, fascist headquarters and the barracks. We were each armed with one 1,000 lb (453 kg) bomb and maximum trays of .5 inch (12.7 mm) bullets with a mixture of explosives and tracers. The trip to Macerata was quiet until we approached the target when we were assailed with a barrage of 88 mm ack-ack.

Facing on to the piazza, the town hall was easy to spot. As we expected, there was no sign of life below; everyone took shelter as they heard us approaching. I was the third Shark to dive and enjoyed seeing the leader and his No 2 firing their guns as they went down, as agreed, to keep the opposition heads down as we attacked. The explosive bullet flashes appeared to go right in through the front door and windows of the town hall.

Their bombs exploded down the side of the target, blowing out windows and part of the roof and starting a fire. I followed down, firing my guns as soon as the one in front was out of the firing line, and dropping my bomb into the target area. We pulled up out of our attack and re-formed among the continuing 88 mm defence. We looked down on the target to see a cloud of smoke, some flames and clear evidence of severe damage to the town hall. Our orders were to escort the Mitchell bombers back south to their base,. We could see the barrack area well trounced and the Mitchells turning away from the target, so we formed up above them to carry out our instructions, glad to be leaving the area.

The rest of the trip also went to plan and we got back to base without loss, although two Kittys had some ack-ack shrapnel damage. The great news came the next day when the 'Y' Service passed on a message to us from the partisans to say what a success the raid had been. Several top Jerry officers and their Fascist cohorts had been killed and many injured, they said. The partisans had been told of our impending attack and had kept clear, so they suffered no casualties. The bombers had also done a good job and demolished the barracks, however, the partisans reported, most of the German soldiers were elsewhere at the time.

I have often wondered what was the full story of events on the ground. It raised so many questions, the answers to which I shall probably never know – intriguing! (See Epilogue for some of the answers). This operation stuck in my mind more than others because it was the only one I can remember where we were ordered to attack the enemy in a civilian area.

On 4 April we heard that our CO, Peter Illingworth had survived and was on his way back to the Squadron. He turned up, weary, footsore, sunburnt and lousy. Apart from that he was in good spirits. He had landed in a stony field and hidden in a dry stone wall with German soldiers walking along the top. Having been seen by the locals they sent children at night with food. Next day the Yugoslavian partisans took him into their care and set about returning him to Italy. They did offer to let him stay and fight with them but he declined with thanks. Peter said he marched and marched hour after hour. He slept in a bed with ten partisans, mostly womenfolk and he said it would have been more comfortable but for the belts of grenades they wore at all times. These partisans put him on a flying boat and returned him to Bari.

Now we had two COs. This problem was resolved the very next day when the Squadron, led by Squadron Leader Watts, set out for an armed recce near Rieti. I was leading the top six. All of us, except apparently the CO, knew the flak situation in this area. We carried long range belly tanks and 40 pounders (18 kg) under the wings. Nearer the target we split up into two sixes and went down to strafe MT. As we got down we could see dozens of MT just off the road under the trees and other camouflage. The flak was intense and we were therefore surprised that the CO led us to strafe many times in the same area. The flak got worse as the Jerries got all their guns firing. It was a mistake to strafe too long in the same defended area. However, we left twenty or so MT and supply dumps all burning.

On pulling away the CO was hit at about 3,000 ft (914 m). His glycol poured out in a stream and he turned back towards base. We stuck around. He called up on the R/T to say he was about to bale out and gave a message for his wife: "Not to worry. Will be back in a month". He flew only a few miles before baling out near Todi. I circled around to see him land safely in a coppice, leave his parachute and run, waving to me as he went.

My six travelled on and found some railway trucks, which we bombed with our 40 pounders from about 500 ft (1524 m), then more MT, which we strafed, leaving ten or fifteen all burning. Apparently they contained fuel and ammo because the explosions and smoke rose to over a thousand feet. Apart from the loss of our new CO it was a very successful day. It was one of our longest trips, taking two hours and forty-five minutes in the air and we had used up all our bombs and ammunition. We claimed over thirty vehicles destroyed or damaged as well as the loss to the Jerries of large supplies of fuel and ammunition.

Next day I led a flight of six Sharks on our own to bomb a factory with our 500 lb (226 kg) bombs. Most fell on the target and we were lucky there was no opposition at all. This time we were only fifty minutes in the air.

I was very excited when the CO, now Peter Illingworth again, asked me to lead the whole squadron of twelve Kittys into battle. The target was a bridge over the river Spoleto. There was no ack-ack as we approached the target so we dive-bombed carefully. All twelve bombs appeared to land on or near the target but it wasn't demolished and we couldn't see, from where we were, at about 3,000 ft (914 m), if we had done much damage. I instructed the other ten Kittys, as pre-planned, to circle and wait while I and my No 2 went down to about 200 ft (60 m) over the bridge to see what we had achieved. The results were good and it was going to take the Jerries some time to repair the railway line and make the bridge safe enough to take a train over. I climbed up and led the Squadron back to base. I felt a great sense of achievement as we came in to land, all safe.

Earlier in April, when unfortunately I was not flying, the full squadron surprised some twelve or more Fw 190s on Rieti landing ground. Some were taxying, taking off or just airborne. A terrific battle ensued and several Fw 190s were destroyed but we lost two Flight Sergeants, one shot down by defending flak and the other trying to do a stall turn back to the landing ground in his excitement. He spun in and blew up. So it was not surprising that our Shark Squadron became temporarily short of pilots at about this time.

CO Peter Illingworth taxiing to the take off point. On the ground it was impossible for the pilot to see clearly, hence the airman on the wing giving directions

CHAPTER TWENTY - ONE

TOUR EXPIRED

One of our flight Commanders, 'Happy' Ahern, was promoted to Squadron Leader, made CO of the Squadron and awarded the DFC. I was promoted to Flight Lieutenant and temporarily put in charge of 'A' Flight.

In mid-April we were re-equipped with Kittyhawk Mk IVs instead of the expected Mustangs. These Kitty IVs had bomb racks to carry a 1,000 pounder (453 kg) under the belly and a 500 pounder (226 kg) under each wing. I did a test flight and found them not much different from the IIIs I had become used to, but there were some teething problems. To rub it in, on 15 April we were escorted by 260 Squadron who were now flying Mustangs. I was flying my new Mk IV 'Z'. The previous one, that had seen me through so much, was the one that had spun in at Rieti. Our target was a railway bridge over the river Fabriano. On the way my R/T system became unserviceable and I had to hand over leadership to Warrant Officer Swinton and become his No 2. This was the first teething problem with the new aircraft. We had two direct hits on the bridge, otherwise the sortie was uneventful.

Next I led the whole Squadron again to a bridge, this time over the river Tiber, sixty miles north of Rome. We left the bridge slightly damaged and flew through some 40 mm flak. We were escorted by four Spitfires and enjoyed liasing with them over the R/T to re-form on the way back. On the 17th we did the same again to a nearby bridge. This time there was no ack-ack but the Spits saw some Me 109s up in the sun and got excited at the prospect of a dog-fight but the enemy cleared off when they realized the magnitude of our formation and escort. It says laconically in my log-book: "No dice". We really smashed up the bridge this trip – the only time I saw a conclusive result from our attacks on bridges.

On the 19th I led the whole Squadron to yet another bridge. There was only slight inaccurate Breda so I went down low with No 2 and saw little damage, only one clean hole from a direct hit that had not exploded. I reckoned it was my bomb because, on checking, I realized I hadn't armed it before going down. So Jerry would have problems with an unexploded bomb under the bridge. However, I kept quiet about it – not being a good example to my colleagues. If I had armed the bomb it could have demolished the bridge... On the way back I was advised by 'Commander' that there was a strong cross wind at Cutella making landing dangerous, so I took the Squadron down to land at a nearby strip called Madna where we hung around till evening when the wind dropped and we could fly to Cutella – a few minutes hop.

On the 20th we flew each with two 500 pounders (226 kg) under the wings and a long range belly tank to San Benedetto to bomb the port buildings. There was heavy 40 mm and 20 mm flak but all came back safely. Early next morning I led the full Squadron with belly tank and no bombs, to strafe MT. We found very little to shoot at. Jerry was a past master at hiding his vehicles in the daytime. The whole Squadron of twelve Kittys and only one flamer to report – I was very disappointed. I had to fly again the same day due to a shortage of pilots. I was not leading and anyway had trouble with the engine cutting every now and again so had to return to base without reaching the target. Was afraid colleagues would think I was getting scared but Nick confirmed that the engine needed attention.

I had one more bridge sortie without incident then to the last trip of the month. I was supposed to lead but again had trouble with my Kitty Mk IV 'Z', FT921. This time the electrics had packed up and I had to hand over to someone else and land without leaving the circuit.

The policy in fighter Squadrons was to consider a tour completed by about 200 operational hours flying before being sent off for a rest. At this time I had flown 193 hours 55 minutes and 128 sorties, so I began to think about a rest. I had shut my mind to the possibility of surviving this tour or not, but as I got near to 200 hours I began to wish fervently to survive and maybe it began to affect my performance. We all knew, without talking about it, that the chance of completing a tour without being killed or taken POW was about 50/50. The Squadron policy was for the CO to end someone's tour when the 200 hours was approaching rather than make a pilot lose concentration knowing it was the last op of the tour. So I was pleased when the CO said: "That's about it, Bert. You are now due for a rest". I didn't show my excitement or huge relief in front of other pilots because they had a lot more to do and it would be unfair. I was packing my things into my suitcase and kit bag on 1 May when I got the message to see the CO. He said "Bert, we're short of pilots and I want you to do one or two more trips". I suppose I said weakly; "Yes, sir, of course". I had a terrible sinking feeling. This was not good for my nerves or morale but I had to do what I was asked (told?).

On 2 May I led the top six to bomb railway lines near Goligno. I had more trouble with my 'Z' but completed the trip this time. The aileron trim was not operating properly, making the lateral control very heavy. Apart from that, it was a routine trip. All I could think about was getting back safely. The next day I spent some time with my rigger working on the aileron. I took it up for a test flight but it was still not flying correctly. I reported to the CO who said: "Probably just one more trip, Bert. You can lead the Squadron in Kitty 'B' tomorrow". I wondered if this was really to be my last trip.

On 4 May, flying 'B', I led the Squadron each with two 500-pounders (226 kg) and a belly tank to railway lines near Spoleto. We got four hits out of twenty-four bombs with little opposition. My bomb was well off target I knew – probably not concentrating! I went down with No 2 to view the damage. The four hits had torn up a long stretch of track and a small bridge had slight damage. Modestly successful, you could call it. I spotted some MT on a village street nearby. I did a quick strafing run, my No 2 strafing also. We left one flamer. Some light flak came up at us from nearby so we cleared off smartly and re-formed with the circling ten Kittys. I led the Squadron back to Cutella and made a careful landing. All were home safely.

This time the CO assured me I had finished my tour. I had flown 130 operational sorties. I packed my things and was sent on my way by truck to Naples and comparative safety.

The Squadron flat in Naples had become very busy. Not only Shark pilots but several Italian hangers-on were always about and there seemed to be a permanent queue of local 'ladies' outside offering to do anything for a good meal. It wasn't as good as it had been when I first visited. There was not much food available in the city except at prices the locals found difficult to afford. We brought basic rations from our Squadron supplies and augmented it with some local delicacies. The 'ladies' were looked on with great suspicion as everywhere in the city were notices asking: "Is VD one of your souvenirs of Naples?"

The seafront at Naples from our flat

My official posting was to the Cocumella Hotel in Sorrento, which was an Aircrew Officers' Rest and Transit centre. This may sound luxurious, and indeed the surroundings were most congenial, but the peacetime hotel furniture had been put into storage and we managed with iron bedsteads and palliasses. I met up with my old CO, Peter Illingworth, and stayed close because, as a senior officer, he had the use of a 13-cwt truck which was essential. So I 'lived' mainly at Sorrento awaiting a posting or embarkation order to England.

Author at the Cocumella Hotel, Sorrento

One day I was with Peter in the truck near Naples when we came across a large encampment of internees consisting of captured Germans and also many Italian civilians all awaiting 'screening' before being sent to POW camps and elsewhere or simply released. We gazed through the wire fence and to our amazement saw our own Stan Worbey in ragged civilian clothes. He was one of our Shark pilots having been shot down sometime earlier as already mentioned. He came waving to the fence when he saw us and shouted: "For God's sake get me out of here! I need a witness before they will believe who I am". We quickly contacted the army Major who was the security officer in charge and he was only too glad to have one of his problems solved. As he said "How can I be sure who's telling the truth – everyone wants out of here!"

As we put Stan into the truck, a column of German army POWs came slouching by. When one of them saw Stan he gave him an ugly look and shook his fist menacingly at him. We wondered what it was all about. We took Stan for a good Italian black-market meal and to hear his story over a bottle or two of Lacrima Christi. His story went something like this.

After he was shot down uninjured but on the wrong side of the bomb-line, he evaded the Germans for some time. He teamed up with a British army sergeant who was equally determined to get back to Allied lines. The difficulty was actually penetrating the front line without getting caught by the Jerries or shot by Allied soldiers. They had a go but were picked up by the Jerries who aimed to transport them back to Germany as POWs. In the event the Jerries imprisoned them overnight in a wooden hut on a hillside with two armed soldiers to ensure they didn't escape. However, one soldier had to leave to go and get food. After seeing this weak spot the sergeant waited till one was away then jumped on the remaining Jerry. He had been trained in commando skills and knew how to kill with a good grip around the throat. This he did and when the Jerry was dead they made their escape before the other returned. As did many evaders, they dug themselves in close to the front line, waited till the Allies advanced over them and then bobbed up on the right side. This time they made it and ended up in the internment camp at Naples.

The incredible coincidence was that the Jerry who had left them to get food and who came back to find his colleague dead, was himself taken prisoner and had seen Stan climbing into our truck. The Jerry's animosity to Stan was quite understandable. However he was now the POW and couldn't do anything except shake his fist.

Stan had another story to tell. During his attempt to get back to our side he had taken a ride in an Italian civilian bus. On his way, the bus was attacked by his own 112 Shark Squadron and his description of being on the receiving end of a strafing attack was horrendous. The bus passengers had run away beyond the side of the road leaving the bus and other MT to catch the full force of our .5-inch (12.7 mm) bullets. Also, the Shark's mouth with ferocious teeth tearing down upon them had been very frightening.

While we sat over the table we remarked that we all had our wrist watches on the inside of the left wrist. The reason was that a Kittyhawk throttle on the left of the cockpit, was close to the metal frame of the fuselage and the action on the throttle scratched and scored any watch on the outside of the wrist. It was a habit we got into which lasted years. If you ever come across someone wearing his wristwatch on the inside of his left wrist – ask him if he flew P-40 Kittyhawks.

I acquired a bout of malaria and ended up in the RAF hospital at

Torre Annunciate at the foot of Mount Vesuvius. Who should be looking after me but Doc Eberle who had been the Shark Squadron MO. He said he could cure me of the malaria because it was not the recurring type but he said I would always have ear trouble after all that dive-bombing. He was right. It couldn't be good for our ears to be diving from 8,000 ft or 9,000 ft (2438 - 2743 m) down almost to ground level in a few seconds.

While recuperating in that hospital a fellow patient and the padre said we should take the opportunity to scale Vesuvius and look down into its crater. I was feeling a bit groggy and only got half way, leaving the other two to go on to the top while I brewed up some tea on the padre's primus stove. It reminded me that while we were at Bari on the east coast we had the experience of being rained on by mud. Very mucky it was too. Vesuvius had erupted and the clouds had carried the debris all the way to the other side of Italy. Now Vesuvius was reasonably quiet.

The author on the slopes of Mt. Vesuvius

I went back to the Cocumella at Sorrento for a while. I was told I was to be sent back to England on the next available boat – whoopee! I had two wonderful weeks waiting for the boat – all relaxed. I did the usual tourist things, the best of which was to take Peter Illingworth's truck along the coast road to Amalfi. It was a bit hairy negotiating blown up bridges with just planks across but the beauty of this coast line will remain with me always.

The Amalfi drive

Another day several of us pilots, together with some lovely PMRAFNS ladies (Princess Mary's Royal Air Force Nursing Service) hired a yacht and boatman for the day. He took us to the isle of San Paulo. We couldn't get near enough to walk ashore so anchored in the little bay and swam ashore for a wonderful Italian picnic, all in blazing sunshine. I also went to Pompeii and Capri. I went into the blue grotto at Capri and to San Michele but didn't enjoy it too much as the Yanks had taken over the island and it was full of the sound of low quality jazz and pop music. It is still too commercialised today!

The time came to board His Majesty's Troopship Orontes in Naples harbour, for the trip back through the Med to England. This journey was far different from the troopship going out to South Africa. There was little danger of enemy attack, the officers' quarters were comfortable and there were many tales of adventure to listen to. Many of the passengers had escaped or evaded the enemy and in recompense were being allowed home. Each had a fascinating story to tell. I questioned and listened all the way back to 'Blighty'.

The Orontes docked at Greenock and I stood looking out over the green fields of Scotland. There had been no greenery to compare anywhere I had been. I decided green would be my favourite colour for life. I noticed that I was not the only one with tears streaming down his face.

I had been overseas three years and a few days. Next, I went to a transit camp for rail tickets, ration books, etc, then on the train to home which was now in Wellingborough, Northamptonshire. I had been home only a few days when the parcel service delivered a kitbag – it was the one I thought had dropped into the Red Sea back in Port Taufiq in July 1942!

CHAPTER TWENTY-TWO

PLOTTING TO FAIL

I waited at home enjoying life but keen to know where I would be posted next and to do what? It was customary to make a tour-expired pilot an instructor at an OTU where he could pass on all the skills he had acquired on a squadron. I was disappointed when eventually the posting came through to send me to Training Command. I reported to 21(P) AFU (Advance Flying Unit) at Wheaton Aston half way between Wolverhampton and Stafford to be 'converted' on to twin engine Oxfords with the intention of making me an instructor. I did about ten hours flying Oxfords. I found them easy to fly once I got used to the effects of having two throttles. They were slow and stolid and aerobatics were quite out of the question – not allowed. Steep turns were the most exciting manoeuvre. A spin was fatal. I also missed the camaraderie of squadron life. Most of the pilots disappeared in the evenings leaving the mess like a morgue.

To become an instructor I had to be properly trained, of course, and to this effect I was sent all the way to Montrose on the east coast of Scotland to No 2 FIS (Flying Instructors School). More Oxford hours together with big chunks of the instructor's handbook to be learnt by heart. I had a colleague from the Shark Squadron, Reg Drown, there on the same course and we plotted to get a posting back on to operations. Each pilot was to have a final test with the CFI (Chief Flying Instructor) before qualifying as an instructor and it was our intention to do all the preliminary work but do badly at the test and so fail to be an instructor. Then we would wheedle our way back on to a squadron.

The weather at Montrose was unlike anything I had experienced. Great layers of fog would lie out to sea leaving the aerodrome in sunshine, only to find a few minutes later that the wind had shifted and that the fog – called haar – had moved in, making flying quite dangerous. We used to say: "Haar, bloody haar, that foxed you!" There was to be an exercise to rescue someone from his inflatable dinghy out to sea. An instructor pilot volunteered to be taken out by boat and left in a dinghy a mile or so out. An Oxford would be sent to make a systematic search until it located the dinghy. Then its location would be radioed back to an Air-Sea Rescue Launch from Montrose harbour, which would go out and 'rescue' the instructor. All a good learning exercise. All went well until the instructor was left out on his own and the Oxford set out to search. Then there was trouble. The dreaded haar moved in and there was no way the Oxford could visually locate the dinghy. The instructor was supposed to be out to sea only an hour or so. In the event the fog hung around and it was twenty-four hours before a worried Oxford and Air-Sea Rescue launch actually rescued him.

We trainee instructors thought it a great joke. The rescued instructor received a great deal of teasing especially when, a few days later, he was awarded the AFC! This award was for years of professional standard instructing but we teased him that he had received it for his night out in the haar.

At the end of the course, consisting of over 100 hours flying, Reg Drown and I faced up to the CFI's flying test. Reg did well – he failed the course and was sent on to more exciting flying elsewhere. The CFI, a Squadron Leader Smith, made me go through the various exercises with quotes from the instructor's handbook and I felt I had done sufficiently badly to fail.

The CFI made no comment till we were back in his office. Then this shrewd man summed up the situation. He said he knew perfectly well that I didn't want to be an instructor but there was a war on and we all had to do our duty and we couldn't pick and choose our work. Our duty was to serve the King and, through our senior officers, serve the RAF to the best of our ability whatever we were asked to do, etc, etc. I felt very small and ashamed. To cap it all he gave me 'Above Average' as a pilot but 'Below Average' as an instructor, stamped permanently in my log book.

Back at Wheaton Aston 21(P) AFU as a fully fledged instructor, life was not difficult. Many of my pupils were ex-instructors from Canada and other parts of the Empire Air Training Scheme, and had flown thousands of hours on Oxfords. They were on their way to operational squadrons, subject to passing through this AFU refresher course. Most of them knew far more than I about flying Oxfords although they had no operational experience at all. Being on multi-engine aircraft they were expecting to go on to Bomber Command. Despite this, we still had to go through all the exercises such as stalling, steep turns, low flying, cross country, navigational tests, swinging the compass, precautionary landings, single engine flying and so on. It was not difficult but rather boring. To brighten up the proceedings I tended to teach them what I could of operational flying instead of the set exercises.

I was put in charge of 'B' Flight, much to the chagrin of other instructors who had been doing the job for many months, if not years, but were still only Flying Officers. I used to arrange solo cross-country exercises for my pupils at weekends, taking them near Sywell Airport which was close to home at Wellingborough. Each exercise had to be approved by the CFI who would not allow any unauthorized landings en route. However, I thought I would go with my pupil and gently drop off at Sywell without anyone knowing, except the pupil of course. This worked fine for three weekends and I persuaded the Sergeant in the control tower at Sywell not to send any confirmatory signal as I wasn't supposed to be there. He was an understanding fellow and all went well.

On the fourth time I tried it, there was a different NCO on duty at Sywell and, misunderstanding my "Please don't send a signal", telephoned instead to Wheaton Aston to say I had landed safely. Unfortunately the CFI was in the control tower at Wheaton Aston at the time and, noting that this was an unauthorized landing, became very hot under the collar right through to Monday, when I returned by rail. He gave me a severe reprimand and said that, just because I had done a tour of ops, I thought I knew it all and could do what I liked... I had to discontinue my free transport home and take a train instead when I wanted to get to Wellingborough – not nearly as convenient!

Many pupils came and went on their way. They were all interesting characters and grateful for the way they were treated. One, whose father had a jewellers shop in Rugby, gave me a set of solid silver coffee spoons, a very great luxury for they were not being made in war-time, with thanks for seeing him successfully through the course.

One day I was flying with a pupil in an Oxford. For some reason we were coming out of a steep drive and therefore near maximum speed when, to my amazement, a Wellington bomber, with its propellers stopped, overtook us, whizzing past at high speed. I blinked and wondered if I had had too much to drink the previous evening. I mentioned this in the mess that evening. Everyone looked around embarrassed. One pilot took me on one side and told me that a secret new engine called a 'jet' had been invented and that it was being tested out in the tail of a Wellington. Having been overseas, this was the first time I had heard of a jet. I was told not to talk about it. 'Careless talk costs lives' as the slogan was in those war days.

Sundays, when I was working, was the day we had to co-operate with the local ATC (Air Training Corps). Their members wanted to fly in the back of our Oxfords. There was room for four of them. My pupils and I proceeded with flying exercises. The big problem was that the Oxford was like a greenhouse, very hot indeed when the sun shone. The ATC boys, keen as they were to fly, were mostly airsick. So it was that I would allow no cadet to enter the aircraft without a large towel. They would protest that they were sure they would be man enough to cope without a towel but I put my foot down. Even so the stench was very unpleasant at times.

One sunny morning I heard that 'A' Flight was going to do some formation flying with five Oxfords. I thought it would be good if we, that is 'B' Flight, did the same. There might be some fun to be had. I saw 'A' Flight take off. We followed shortly after, climbing up until I could see 'A' Flight formation, very neat and proper, in the distance. I led my formation of five Oxfords till we were above the others and up in the sun. Then we dived down out of the sun on the unsuspecting formation below. It was a wonderful sight. They scattered all over the sky in total disarray. They must have thought we were Jerry fighters! All my pupil pilots enjoyed it enormously. It was the first bit of excitement they had had. Eventually we all landed and I returned to my Flight office to hear the phone ringing. It was the CFI to tell me that he had decided to go formation flying with 'A' Flight that morning and had led the formation until some fool out of the sun, broke up his formation. He presumed it was me. As instructed, I reported to his office to be told: "Just because you have been on ops you think you know it all and can do what you like. Well you can't here!"

He said he didn't want me on his station and I could go home till he arranged a fresh posting to be sent to me. I had about ten days at home before the telegram arrived. I was to go to No 1 Beam Approach School at Watchfield to become a Blind Flying Instructor. It sounded more interesting than what I had been doing but was still in Training Command.

CHAPTER TWENTY-THREE

BLIND FLYING

At Watchfield I learned the Beam Approach and Instrument Landing System and how to fly around the country in ten-tenths cloud using a system of beams. Also, I learned how to teach these systems to others. I enjoyed this flying quite a lot. There was some excitement in landing an Oxford completely blind. There was a hood to unfurl over the pupil in good weather and in any case we were expected to fly in all weather conditions.

The principle generally was that, heading in the right direction, the pilot heard a steady note on the R/T. If he veered to the left he heard a series of dit-dit-dits and if he veered off to the right got a series of dah-dah-dahs. Coming in to land there were two radio beacons on the approach making a rapid series of dahs or dits as we flew over them. There was a correct height to be at as we passed over them coming in to land. The expert pilot could then feel gently with the wheels until he touched down on the tarmac.

I enjoyed this blind flying and the sense of achievement: taking off, flying around the country on the beams, finding an aerodrome with the ILS (Instrument Landing System) and landing safely – all without seeing outside the cockpit. I got an 'Above Average' in my log book for Beam Approach flying.

The war in Europe was approaching its end and the dozens of airfields in the UK were being evaluated for their usage. Consequently, some were shutting down and I found myself posted from aerodrome to aerodrome – all the time instructing a succession of pilots how to fly blind.

I did some instructing at Coleby Grange, Lincolnshire, then at Wymeswold near Loughborough. At this aerodrome the Navy were practicing landing on an Aircraft Carrier Deck marked out on the grass. I tried a few landings myself and fell off the 'end of the ship' a few times before getting the hang of it. I developed a great respect for Navy flyers. Then to Chipping Warden near Banbury, finally coming to rest at St Mawgan near Newquay in Cornwall. I flew from St Mawgan for a six-month period. There I developed a great sense of camaraderie among the other instructors and, as the pupils came and went, they enjoyed it also. Some of my pupils were civilian BOAC (British Overseas Airways Corporation) pilots on refresher courses.

The visibility at St Mawgan could be almost non-existent as mists rolled in off the sea. Still we flew in all weather conditions regardless, on the principle that we were teaching our pupils to fly blind – we should be able to do it in 'real life' – and we did. In good weather we drew the hood over the pupil and let him have a go. In this case the instructor could, of course, see any problems with a normal view of the proceedings.

I made friends with an instructor called Stan who happened to come from my home town of Wellingborough. At every possible opportunity he went off to see his Wren girl-friend just up the coast at a Navy land station. The whole staff there were Wrens and the Wren officer in charge was a real 'battleship' in her own right and very protective of her 'girls'. It occurred to me that if I could 'shoot up' this Wren encampment without letting the 'battleship' see my aircraft registration letters, Stan would be an immediate suspect as he had his girlfriend there. Therefore, one fine day when Stan had gone up with a pupil in his Oxford doing the usual exercises, my pupil and I climbed into our Oxford and set out for the Naval station.

There is a special skill in flying low over and diving upon a target without those on the ground getting a chance to record the registration letters painted on the side of the fuselage. As we flew over the camp the Wrens came out to see what was going on and suitably ducked as we whipped smartly over their rooftops, just missing the chimneys. After a while we made our way back to St Mawgan and continued with the exercises of the day as if nothing had happened.

I must have done a good job. The 'battleship' was furious. She phoned our CO at St Mawgan and accused him of letting one of his Oxfords perpetrate this terrible offence. He, of course, promised to bring the offender to justice. His first choice, as expected, was Stan who, of course, proclaimed his innocence with great fervour. I promise you that if Stan were to be punished I would definitely have owned up and taken the consequences. But it all worked perfectly. Stan could prove, with his pupil as a witness, that he hadn't been near the Navy camp at all. Fortunately the 'battleship' did not have the registration letters of the offending aircraft, so our CO came to a dead end. Some of the other instructors suspected that I was the culprit but they and my pupil did not give me away. After a few days all the uproar died down, no one was punished and it wasn't till a good year later that, as civilians at Stan's wedding (yes, the same Wren), I admitted to him that it was I who beat up the Wren's quarters in Cornwall. He forgave me.

The war was over – thank goodness. Great celebrations!

My story tells only of my experiences. It says nothing of the heart-broken mothers, fathers, sweethearts and families, the tears, the pain and discomfort the war caused for millions of people throughout the world. The blame rested with the German people and the wicked, wicked Hitler and his henchmen in particular. The war was not of our choosing but, once into it, all the individual could do was his or her best to bring it to a correct conclusion. That's what thousands of us in the RAF did to the best of our ability.

If this sounds like a glorification of war, you are wrong. Our humour, excitement and dedication saw at least some of us through to the end. We needed to have this psychological approach to our job here described to cope at all. Those that died so we could enjoy freedom and, hopefully, some peace will not be forgotten. This book is dedicated to them.

Shortly after the Wren episode the RAF decided not to avail themselves of my services any longer and I went for 'de-mob'. Everyone leaving the RAF had to have a medical examination so as not to burden the authorities with pensions for life if it could be avoided by them. When the MO (Medical Officer) saw my varicose veins in my legs he quite rightly reckoned they had developed from pushing the rudder pedals while dive-bombing. He insisted that I should have this minor operation to get rid of them, avoiding them developing into something painful for me and expensive for the RAF. I was posted to RAF Hospital Locking, near Southend-on-Sea for this operation. Then I went for a free civilian suit and rail ticket home.

As my Squadron MO foretold, I have very sensitive ears. Even the change in height up and down hills in a car or in a lift gives me pain. In an airliner it is very acute. I'm not grumbling. I survived and everything else seems unimportant.

I had completed, with the RAF, 1,114 hours flying time. Not many compared with some others but I enjoyed every minute in the air and most of the time on the ground – especially my 130 operations with the Shark Squadron.

EPILOGUE

MACERATA - NOVEMBER - 1996

GUEST OF HONOUR

When I opened the letter I guessed it would be bad news, but I wasn't expecting it to be so bad - 110 casualties. It didn't say how many were killed, but there must have been many. My first thought was that, after 52 years, there was nothing to be done about it, but as the days went by, thinking of little else, I determined that something should be done.

On 2nd April 1944 an RAF squadron of single-seat Kittyhawk fighter-bombers was stationed around a landing strip called Cutella, on the Adriatic coast just north of the "spur" of Italy and used for dive-bombing and strafing the gradually retreating German forces. It was known as the Shark Squadron for its menacing shark's teeth painted on the nose. The Italian government had capitulated to the Allies some six months previously and some of the population had turned against the Germans and become active underground partisans, others sided with them as Fascist militia.

I was a pilot of the Shark Squadron and was being briefed for the following day's work. We heard from the partisans via the secret radio listening service, that a meeting of top German generals with their Fascist friends was to take place in the Town Hall at Macerata at 11 am on the following morning. We had been ordered to attack this building at exactly that time and the partisans were to attack the Germans later.

So, on the 3rd April 1944, eleven Kittyhawks took off into the morning sunshine. The town was just over half an hour's flight along the coast and a few miles inland, south of Ancona. Our squadron leader found a building facing the piazza and manoeuvred into an attacking position. I was the third aircraft to dive, strafing and dropping a 1000 lb (435kg) bomb. I saw the first two bombs drop on the building, blowing out windows and doors.

We re-formed and headed for base and all returned safely, the whole operation had taken just under two hours. The next day we were told briefly that according to the partisans the raid had been 'a success' but for two reasons this operation remained on my mind. Firstly, I had a few unanswered question: How did the partisans hear about the meeting? How did they fare with their attack after we were gone? Did we kill the German generals? What happened to the civilians? Secondly, it was our only operation on a civilian occupied target. The others had been on enemy positions, motor transport, shipping, bridges, railways, aircraft in the air and on the ground.

Now, 52 years later, I stood with my wife Christine on the cobbled piazza in the medieval town of Macerata looking up at the balcony of the Town Hall surrounded by buildings in soft brown brickwork. The Town Hall itself was a three-storey building, the ground floor faced with six square pillars supporting the balcony above - and no sign of any bomb damage. At the time of our attack many townsfolk would have been killed or injured. Their families would remember only too well. What would be the reaction to our visit? We couldn't blame them if it was to be extremely cool. In a few minutes we were to meet Giuseppe Ghergo, a highly respected doctor in the town, and his wife Virginia. Giuseppe had been the one to write that letter. He was a boy of twelve in the town at the time of the raid and was now writing its history. He had wanted to be in contact with a pilot who flew with the Shark Squadron on 3rd April 1944. His letter of August 1996 was my first contact with anyone of Macerata.

On that fateful day Giuseppe had been standing on the balcony of his home watching our Kittyhawks dive down and hearing the roar of the bombs, before his mother pulled him away to the air-raid shelter. He remembered clearly the third Kittyhawk to dive. I was the 23 year old pilot of that aircraft. His letters disclosed that the 11am meeting did not take place. If it had ever existed it had been called off and could have been an excuse created by the partisans to persuade the RAF to bomb the town for their own ends. They were under constant German and Fascist attack, assaults, fights and killings were common and only two weeks previously twenty three partisans had been shot at a nearby town. No partisan attack followed the bombing.

The casualties of our bombing numbered 110: 15 Italian and 2 German soldiers, together with 93 civilians.The thought of all these casualties made me despair. I could not say sorry for the raid, only for the outcome. After all, our Squadron would do the same again in similar circumstances, but perhaps we could make a gesture of peace to the present population of Macerata.

Then the story took another twist when I received a copy of a letter from the Foreign and Commonwealth Office who, after consulting their archives in London, suggested the raid had not been in vain after all. It read, *"The raid on 3rd of April 1944 was on Macerata prison and it result-ed in the escape of a British officer who is believed to have been a member of M19 (the escape organization) and a number of Italian partisans who had been condemned to death and were awaiting execution"*. I realized then that the true reason for the raid may never be known.

My thoughts continued regarding a gesture towards Macerata and our "Shark Squadron Association" gave it their blessing. Christine directed me to a local sculptor who had a design for a work called "Unity". This was something the squadron could do for Macerata.

Unity was commissioned and I set about composing the wording for its brass plaque. The sculpture was to be about 20 centimetres high in bronze resin and was of a group of figures young and old with their arms around each other. I could have sent it by courier to the Mayor with a letter of explanation, but something inside asked, why don't you take it? Whatever reception would I get - the bomber meeting the results of his bombs face to face?

After telephone calls to Giuseppe, a meeting was agreed for the 30th November 1996. Christine and I were going to Macerata to face whatever would be in store for us. Full of concerns we headed for Macerata, arriv-ing at our hotel to find ourselves only a few metres from the piazza. A mes-sage awaited us at reception to say Giuseppe and Virginia would meet us at 11 am, the very hour of our attack in 1944. At the due time we walked out onto the piazza to stand for a few minutes awaiting our meeting. They arrived punctually at 11am and we received a big smiling welcome. It was an historic moment as we shook hands: the bomber and the bombed with no apparent rancour. I began to feel all would be well that day.

The Mayor, Professor Gian M Maulo, was expecting us, so we walked together across the piazza to the Town Hall. A great sense of occasion came over me as we climbed the marble staircase to be met by the Mayor himself; another smiling welcome. He showed us into his inner parlour and I made my one sentence speech in Italian: *"Io porto l'amore, respetto e pace"* (I bring love respect and peace). The mayor then handed me a letter which he had been asked to deliver to me and which, he said, typified the feelings of the people of Macerata.

As I heard the translation I realized it would be the culminating moment of my visit. It read:

MACERATA 30.XI. 1996

*To kind English Aviator. The writer, on the day of
the bombardment was about 10 years old. By a
divine miracle, he did not die. One bomb fell and
exploded about 40 metres away smashing a lot of
buildings but not the old palace where I hid. You
must not blame yourself because you were
ordered. Instead I have to recognize and appreci-
ate your Squadron's beautiful and noble gesture
of peace*

Yours sincerely, ANTONIO GUARNIERE

We unwrapped the sculpture and presented it to the Mayor. He examined it carefully and read the inscription, in Italian, on the brass plaque:

BROTHERHOOD

*This reminds us that, in the face of destructive
forces, human dignity and love will triumph over
disaster and bring nations together in respect
and peace.*

*3rd April 1944. Presented by 112 Squadron RAF
November 1996*

He kissed me on both cheeks and assured me that it would be placed in the Town Library where all citizens could see it and read the inscription. He and I talked about how good often came out of evil. He presented me with a lavishly illustrated book of the beautiful theatre of which they, in Macerata, are so proud; a memento of an emotional but pleasant meeting. As we left the parlour we were met by photographers and journalists thrusting their microphones in my face. They asked; "Why did you not have Spitfire escort?" "Would you do the same again?" and more. At the mayor's suggestion photographs were taken of me standing with him on the balcony overlooking the piazza. Until that moment I had been occupied coping with the conversation and the questions but now it hit me that I was standing on the balcony of the building that had been our wartime target.

Then we said our good-byes and stepped down on to the piazza. A picture came into my mind of the last time I had seen that place as I came roaring down aiming at those pleasant buildings. I pondered the stupidity of war.

During a happy lunch together with Giuseppe and Virginia I was given a memento to take back to England. To my horror it was a lump of jagged metal - part of the casing of a bomb dropped by us on that raid. Virginia hastened to assure me it was given without any bitterness - amazing! I tried to pay our way for lunch but Giuseppe (who professed to not speaking English) had one question ready: "Are you mad?"

Our hosts took us to see the university, the theatre with its marble decor and an open-air opera house of international fame. Our tour included sight of buildings that had been occupied by the Fascists and German officers, some damaged by our bombs and gunfire.

We drove next day to Bologna airport and so back home. We had been in the house only five minutes when the telephone rang. It was Virginia to make sure we were safely back home. All this kindness and understanding surely bodes well for mankind.

As Giuseppe wrote: The 3rd April 1944 was indeed a tragic day for the town, but no ill-feeling was felt towards the attackers but rather towards those who had prompted the action. On the other hand the partisans too are to be excused (the French have a saying; *"a la guerre comme a la guerre"*), even if they must have known there would be innocent victims.

Author with the restored Me109G, Black 6, on its arrival at the Imperial War Museum, Duxford, August 1991. This aircraft was forced down by a Shark Squadron pilot in the Western Desert. Its pilot, Heinz Ludemann, managed to evade capture and returned to his unit to fly again. However, just a few months later he was again shot down by a pilot from 112 Squadron and was killed

*At the time of writing the first draft of 'Shark Squadron Pilot' this Me 109G
was the only airworthy German aircraft which had seen active service in
World War two. Sadly, after only a few air display seasons, it was involved in a
near fatal accident at Duxford and the decision was made to only return it to
'static display', rather than 'flying' standard when it was repaired*

INDEX

Note: Because they change, ranks have been omitted

St. Mawgan, Cornwall   178 179
Safi, Malta   87
Salerno, Italy   122
Salisbury, Rhodesia   29
San Benedectio, Italy   164
San Giovanni, Italy   117
San Michele, Capri, Italy   170
San Paulo, Italy   170
Sara, Italy   149
Savoia-Marchetti   67 68 82 123
Sawman, N.Africa   83
Sfax, Tunisia   69 76
SFTS   26 28 108
Shadow Firing   44
Sharp N, SAAF   140
Shaw, 'Artie' RCAF   102
Shepheards Hotel   36
Sibenik, Yugoslavia   140
Siebel Ferries   117
Sinkat   41
Skip Bombing   117 118
Smith CFI   173
Smith, Engineer   126
Snaddon, Russ   54
Sopwith Camels   59
Sorrento, Italy   166 170
Soru, Italy   141
Spam   67 138
Sphinx   33
Spinazola, Italy   122
Spoletto, Italy   161 165
Splash Targets   28
Stalag Luft III (Sagen – Poland)   54
Staveley W R   122
Starlight Club   31
Stewart, 'Doc'   16 17

OTHER TITLES FROM INDEPENDENT BOOKS

'BLUE SKIES AND DARK NIGHTS'

By

Bill Randle

ISBN: 1 872836 40 2

'Blue Skies and Dark Nights' is the autobiography of Group Captain Bill Randle. From his initial flight training in the United States on the fledgling Arnold scheme, to the bombing of Germany, through a remarkable evasion and successful 'home run', to MI9 and the formation of post-war Escape and Evasion policy with the Americans, to learning to fly helicopters with the US Marines, then on to taking part in search and rescue missions in Korea; this is a honest and straightforward account of a unusual career in the RAF and beyond.

Those with an interest in the RAF and world affairs will find Bill Randle's story fascinating as he describes what it was like to be at the centre of many world events. It also clearly illustrates the frustrations implicit in a service life, as well as the great humour and tragedy which go with the acceptance of the responsibilities of rank.

'Blue Skies and Dark Nights' is an important record of service in the RAF during World War Two and in the 'Cold War' period that followed, together with the great changes in Africa and the declaration of UDI by the erstwhile RAF fighter pilot Ian Smith.

Retiring in 1971 Bill went on to work at the fast growing RAF Museum at Hendon and has gone on to raise a little under six million pounds for Service charities. Now turning his hand to writing, his autobiography is his third book and is both an important story and a delight to read.

Hardback 352 pages 156 x 240 mm. Well illustrated with over ninety previously unpublished photographs.

£19.95

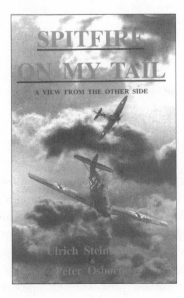

'SPITFIRE ON MY TAIL'

By

Ulrich Steinhilper & Peter Osborne

ISBN 1 873836 003

On 27th October 1940, having completed over 150 missions, Oberleutnant Ulrich Steinhilper's fighter was shot down, crashing into the Kent countryside near Canterbury. For Ulrich that was the end of everything for which he'd been prepared in the *Luftwaffe* since his acceptance in 1936. But there is more than a pilot's story to tell. He shares with the reader what it was like to grow up in Germany as the crippling conditions of the Treaty of Versailles bled away the country's economy; how it was inevitable that the people would succumb to the fatal attraction of Hitler and The Party. And, more personally, how the intrigues and politics of a small town were to shape his destiny.

From a mountain village in southern Germany to Berlin swollen with people for the 1936 Olympic games, we follow Ulrich to the start of his military career and through the rigorous basic training to his first faltering flights as a pilot. Onwards, towards the Battle of Britain and his uncompromising views of the conduct of the battle both by the *Luftwaffe* High Command and the RAF.

In a fighter group decimated by losses and battle fatigue Ulrich still carries on, but is he really prepared for what has befallen his friends and colleagues? If the *Luftwaffe's* estimates of British fighter strength were correct, then why are they still facing such determined resistance? Will the Army ever start the invasion of Britain? Will the sacrifice of so many airmen have been for nothing?

Very well reviewed and now quoted as a 'standard work' on the period in many new titles - a classic.

Hardback, 352 pages, 84 illustrations, 160 x 240 mm

£17.95

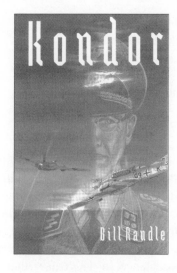

'KONDOR'

By

Bill Randle

ISBN 1 873836 25 9

This exciting new book is largely based on fact, and on the first hand experiences of Bill Randle who, as a young Sergeant Pilot, was shot down whilst flying a Wellington bomber in 1942. What followed forms the basis of this story; Bill, however, has chosen to tell it from a unique perspective.

As the RAF stepped up its bombing campaign in Germany and the Occupied countries, more and more aircrew were falling victim to the steadily increasing number of flak guns and to the nightfighters hunting under the cloak of darkness. Those airmen who survived often managed to evade immediate capture and were able to make contact with the Resistance. Gradually, more and more Allied aircrew were successfully 'processed' and passed down a carefully prepared escape line to a neutral country and eventually back home to fly again.

Acutely aware of this, the Germans strove relentlessly to destroy these lines, together with the courageous people who ran them. This is the fascinating account of one such operation, code-named Kondor: although a novel, the blend of fact and fiction is such that the reader may find difficulty in differentiating between the two...

Harback, fiction, 288 pages, 160 x 240 mm

£14.95

'BROKEN WINGS'

By

Bill Randle

ISBN 1 872836 35 6

Opening in 1914, *'Broken Wings'* introduces Bill's new character, Thomas Ebdon. Fascinated from an early age with the embryonic science of flight, Thomas resolves to become a flyer. However, his humble beginnings in rural Devon dictate that he must serve King and Country in the Infantry and from his idyllic country life he is pitched into the charnel house that is to be the beginning of the First World War.

Fighting in the mud and barbed wire he sees the early bombers and fighters wheeling overhead and yearns to fly, to take the fight to the enemy in the open halls of the sky. At first discouraged because 'only gentlemen fly' he persists and is eventually accepted for the Royal Flying Corps. As he enters the realms of the 'twenty minuters' (the average life expectancy of a new pilot and observer) he finds he is a natural flyer and manages to outlive many of his peers. But as the pressures increase and the armament of the aircraft becomes steadily more deadly how long will he survive?

Calling upon his extensive knowledge of the First World and of early aviation Bill has created another masterpiece historical novel which will keep readers engrossed to the end. 'Broken Wings' is a must for anyone with an interest in the First World War, in aviation or anyone who likes a good story well written.

Hardback, fiction, 224 pages, 160 x 240 mm

£14.95

SIGNED EDITIONS

BATTLE OF BRITAIN 60TH ANNIVERSARY COMMEMORATIVE EDITION

'SPITFIRE ON MY TAIL'

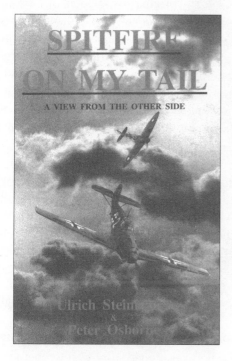

Ulrich Steinhilper's story of this decisive air battle from the German perspective which is now being quoted as a classic work in several new publications.

This is a **limited and numbered edition of the book,** signed on a specially designed book plate by both Ulrich Steinhilper and by Sergeant 'Bill' Skinner who is credited with shooting him down.

Probably the last opportunity to obtain the original signatures of two men who met in aerial combat during this epic struggle.

£29.95

'LAURELS FOR PRINZ WITTGENSTEIN'

By

Werner Roell

Special Signed Edition

Containing a specially designed book plate on which appear six original siganatures of *Luftwaffe* personnel who either flew with Wittgenstein or who knew him well. Five of these are holders of the Knight's Cross and include:

General Günther Rall - the third highest scoring German fighter pilot still alive and the third during WW II.

Major Hajo Herrmann - the inovator of the Wilder Sau night-fighter tactics and probably Germany's most able wartime airman.

Major Wolfgang Falk - one of the leading inovators in night-fighter tactics.

Major Heinz Cramer who was Herrmann Göring's adjutant in 1938 and a highly decorated bomber pilot.

Major Werner Roell the author of the book.

£29.95

UK: £3 Worldwide Surface Mail £3.50 Air Mail at Cost.

INDEPENDENT BOOKS
3 Leaves Green Crescent,
Keston,
Bromley,
BR2 6DN
United Kingdom

Tel: (UK+44) 01959 573360
Fax: UK+44)) 01959 541129

e-mail: mail@independentbooks.co.uk